FORGIVE US OUR SENIOR MOMENTS

FORGIVE US OUR SENIOR MOMENTS

WALTER A. ATKINSON

Elderberry Press, LLC

Copyright © 2002 by Robert W. Hamor

All rights reserved. No part of this publication, except for brief excerpts for purpose of review, may be reproduced, stored in a retrieval system, or transmitted in any form or by any means, electronic, mechanical, photocopying, recording, or otherwise without the prior written permission of the publisher.

❧ Elderberry Press
1393 Old Homestead Drive, Second floor
Oakland, Oregon 97462—9506.
www.elderberrypress.com
TEL/FAX: 541.459.6043

All Elderberry books are available from your favorite bookstore, amazon.com, or from our **24 hour order line: 1.800.431.1579**

Library of Congress Control Number: 2002109540
Publisher's Catalog-in-Publication Data
Forgive Us Our Senior Moments/Walter A. Atkinson
ISBN 1-930859-37-6
1. Conservatism——Nonfiction.
2. Commentary——Nonfiction.
3. Satire——Nonfiction.
4. Humor——Nonfiction.
5. Senior Citizens——Nonfiction.
I. Title

This book was written, printed, and bound in the United States of America.

Dedication

To Helen, my fifty year partner and friend through times good and not so good, who graciously acknowledged the hyperbole in some of these essays to be a whimsical fiction that she could accept and persevere. To Dan C. and Hanna D., my American and Polish attorneys, respectively, who never stopped encouraging. To Fred and Ed and Jane and Owen who contributed to the project, often at times without ever knowing. And to the memory of Cora and Walter Atkinson: the inspirational heart and soul for much of the material contained herein.

Disclaimer

This is a work of non-fiction. Except as otherwise described, all past events and situations are factual. Apart from direct family members, however, characterization and description in this book is at times, preferentially, a composite of actual people and places that I have known.

Contents

Preface..9
1. Ancestors...13
2. Retirement...25
3. Foolin' Around..35
4. Music..43
5. Home Improvement..55
6. Like, Love, Marriage and Then Some..................61
7. Self-Improvement...71
8. Movies..81
9. Religion..93
10. Sports..101
11. Political Bents...115
12. Anomalies..127
13. Look To The Future.......................................143
14. The AARP Be With You: R.I.P. Uncle Bob..........159
Notes...167

Preface

The words comprising this book represent a treatise excerpted from sixty-five years of my life. It is clearly a little about a lot, and not much about anything. In fact, an early title was *Out of My Life and Thought* until I realized that Albert Schweitzer had dibs on that one from some decades back. Not being in Schweitzer's league, I naturally stood down. Many may wonder, then, "So who's this nobody that, just because he turned 'senile citizen,' we should be hanging onto his every syllable?" As Richard Nixon stated many times, "Let me say this about that."

Why not me? My entire existence has been one large tendency to do important things later in life. Many folks call that procrastination; I consider it deferred pre-planning. Logically, since waiting all these years to finally speak out, I should have a great deal to say. At the end of this dissertation, then, I fully expect to be judged as either reasonably convincing, or a frothing, conservative half-wit. The verdict is yours. Many will find my material to be grossly opinionated. Others will take issue with my political stance. I make no apologies. Where convictions differ feel at liberty to consider my view a *senior moment*.

The essays written here share a commonality from the 1930s, 1940s and 1950s, through the year 2000 and beyond. They express our roots and beliefs and attitudes from those times. They say how we lived and, sometimes, why. They speak of our pride in family values, school and church, about respect for women, children, elders and the law of the land. They talk about our regard for something called a work ethic. Bigotry was plentiful, too, in those earlier years, but slowly being exposed and attacked, as it still is today. In 1946 the United States of America was the greatest country that ever existed on the face of the earth. The devastation of a crippling economic depression was behind us. The devil's triumvirate—Nazi Germany, Italy and Japan—had been obliterated in yet another tragic and costly *world war to end all wars*. The Marshall Plan founders were readying programs, on a global scale, to assist in the recovery of war-torn countries. The G. I. Bill of Rights, via direct payments for academic and vocational enrollment, initiated and succeeded in the almost impossible task of educating millions of returning American servicemen.

So, what happened?

A *cultural revolution* happened, I guess; whatever that is. Somewhere along the way our great society delivered the uncommon heritage of many great generations into the hands of the future. In this case, I think, the future dropped it.

These chapters criticize some of today's mainstream social situations. As to a serious solution: none is offered, or even considered. Through various means—humor, irreverence, patriotism, profanity, nostalgia—the attempt is made to expose the incompatibility of core societal issues—today versus yesterday—as part of the insidious moral decline in America which, in turn, preoccupies—for good or bad—the ongoing lifestyle of today's typical senior citizen. It's a life in which most of us are stuck . . . a lifestyle that impacts each of us in different ways, particularly after having revered a past that we had practically molded from our own sweat, blood and guts . . . supposedly for the ages. Possibly—since 9/11—some basics of the "American way" show signs of resurrection.

The pages in this volume are dedicated to the citizens of all years, but mostly to those of the World War II era, an age that easily redefined civilization and humanity. It was an age that experienced constant uncertainty in daily living. Through six years of international conflict there seemed no end, as we continually learned, of new tragedies in the saga of man's inhumanity to man. Simple acceptance of the reality of instant death or injury became routine to many. When considered in its totality, all conflicts before and after World War II almost seem to me now *gentlemanly* in nature. I mention this at the risk of offending many brave veterans.

I have staunch liberal friends who, upon reading these pages, will certainly discover the depths of my conservatism. I hope they will be as *understanding and non-combative to personal feelings* as I have been throughout the *liberal* travesties since the mid-1960s, and more particularly during the 1990s. I refuse any longer to hide my feelings simply for the sake of good order and goodwill toward friends and mankind. In light of the destruction of 9/11, I am certain that additional collateral damage to our government infrastructure will eventually surface and be traced directly to the *aiding and abetting* of the Clinton White House years.

The real Senior Moment, therefore, is not about you or me. It is about entire generations of '30s, '40s and '50s survivors finding themselves in a *today* world not of their making, being hailed as heroes, but treated as bums; accepting lip service from a grateful nation on holidays that are no longer holidays except on long weekends, thanks to the federally mandated Monday Holiday Act; and, finally, praying for the stamina, patience and will to cope a while longer, until the inevitable day of grace takes them home.

WAA

Chapter One

Ancestors

"Did you ever stop to figure that this very life we lead
Was led by our ancestors, don't you know?
We imagine that we're living in an age of mighty speed,
But to tell the truth we're absolutely slow.
For fashions, fads and fancies always are and always were;
Tho' they rave about progression, there's been nothing new occur.
Ev'rything is just the same as when they wrote the calendar,
And that's over nineteen hundred years ago."[1]

My father used to say that our family was kin to a lot of famous or near famous folks. Actually, Dad's real "fifteen minutes of fame" came in 1917 during high school with a classmate who would later become Fred Waring and His Pennsylvanians. Naturally, during those years Fred hadn't even considered forming a band or a glee club. He was just simple, old Fred Waring—and barely known, at that, except around town. During college, according to Dad, Fred was even kicked out of the Penn State freshmen chorus for singing off-key. Later in life, since he and Fred had sung and performed together in a number of high school musicals, Dad always referred to their collaboration as Fred Waring and The Pennsylvanian. Except that Dad never did get invited to Shawnee-on-Delaware. That was Fred's retreat in eastern Pennsylvania where he used to go play golf and work on his blender. Dad was more into horseshoes and ice cubes in a tall glass. He never publicly expressed regret at being disassociated from such potential fame and splendor. During those formative years, Dad's honest attitude regarding Fred Waring was: "I taught him some four-part harmony, a few chords on the piano and uke. I even threw in my old drawings for a hopeless gadget I called The Atkinson Juicer and told him to check back with any problems. The guy'll never do a thing on his own. Count on it!"

As a growing boy in the late 1930s and 1940s everybody's immediate family was about ten thousand times bigger than mine. The size of other families put ours to shame but it was still a burden to keep every relative's name and face in your head, particularly when you didn't see them everyday. It suggested reading a book on royalty, or the Mellon family, or the Rockefellers, where they paste a miniature family tree right inside the cover. Sometimes at outings—in addition to name tags—I fancied a sticky-back placard pasted inside my shirt cuff as a visual aid for pinpointing unfamiliar relatives. Similar to the list of key plays amnesic quarterbacks tape to their wrists, my cheat sheet would smartly identify and briefly describe every name on the family tree. With a sizable tree, my "shirt cuff" method could fill up the whole shirt, as well as my pants. But, think of the instant knowledge, and from a ten year old kid. Such a data bank could easily turn any kid in the clan into the family "smart ass" in record time. Computers came too late. Using concealed laptops at family reunions, we could've been fast tracking marriages and deaths, down loading flow charts on kids and in-laws and first, second and third cousins, other cousins, aunts and uncles through marriage, and plotting graphs on who was famous for awhile, and who was the town drunk, and how did God let the greatest cousin you ever bragged about in your young life get killed on a Sunday morning in 1941 at a place called Pearl Harbor.

The singular thought of ancestors takes me back to "ancient" family photo albums that became an enduring part of my childhood. In our family, most of those pictures depicted German ancestors of the late 1800s and early 1900s. Leafing through old albums provided many a good evening's entertainment. Group shots with actual names and dates written across the back made it even better. Photographers of yore always captured a strangely similar likeness, portraying a staged setting of swarthy Europeans on an outing somewhere in a big, grassy meadow, posing beneath a huge, spreading tree, enjoying those "good old days" amid beer kegs, band instruments and a gang of bewildered kids, boys and girls in the frustrating throes of becoming Americanized, I suppose, as their native German language was gradually falling away. It's easy to imagine the sequence of days behind those faded images locked in time onto a long ago exposed piece of film. Peering back through the years we can follow stoic ancestors who, having just cleared the rigors of immigration, *en masse*, immediately, fervently lock-step aboard the last bus leaving Ellis Island so to reach this precise depicted locale, at this exact moment in time, for the unique purpose of revering a brand new day and freezing it on film forever—a portrait for the ages. Clothes are their Sunday finest. Each face is the look of scrubbed, new life. Clearly, though, the day of the photographer's order to "smile" or "say cheese" is yet to come. The only guy beaming sits next to the keg. The women are seated and look dour. They all seem to wear the same broad-brimmed hat style with the wide band. Their long, heavy skirts touch the ground—covering, no doubt, matronly "combat-like" boots beneath. Bosoms are scrupulously covered—practically up to the lower lip—and pumped to the collar bone with natural fill, curiously resembling a little girl's Halloween imitation of a straw-stuffed, old-maid aunt. All the men there, from the age of shaving on up, sport a beard, sideburns, or a magnificent handle bar moustache. The husbands practically exude distraction as they stand straight and obedient by their *haus fraus*. Hear them moan: *"This picnic is 'no picnic.' Ve belong at our club—at the Liederkranz for the singing unt the drinking unt playing the cards."* And then there is this from those old, faded prints: Each of them, from sixty years and prior, forever presents their own matchless, roguish type clown posing out in front of the assemblage—a centerpiece for posterity—lying right there on the ground as if sponsoring the gathered affair. Usually decked out in a kepi and hoisting a gigantic, foaming mug of beer, this ace among men is always snapped lolling back superciliously onto his side and elbow while peering into the camera with a smug as hell look that says, *"It's mein new homeland, unt any'vheres I vant I lay around."* The children that pose in the captured pastoral beauty are scattered throughout, exposing a simple look of dazed wonderment as they grudgingly pray, no doubt, for the elder's beer and smokes to expire and so, for the real picnic to begin.

Modern day reunions, although less frequent, are larger because more relatives attend. These gatherings take on the drama and expense of major political conventions. Precise coordination is required to meet and conquer endless problems with schedules and physical locations of invited family and friends. There's the planning—committees for food, entertainment, lodgings, facilities, permits, etceteras. And, thanks or no thanks to the Internet, planners now can even ferret out the random family recluse . . . that long lost cousin who wasted his "middle years" posing *incognito,* trying to avoid discovery by the next family reunion "search and seizure" committee. Reunions are truly media events today. In the 1940s, with ten relatives, a case of beer and a banjo uke, reunions happened with the whimsy of picking sides for touch football. Furthermore, with good weather and friendly neighbors, by eight in the evening of the same day one could easily be hosting a full-fledged block party. And we couldn't even spell "committy."

A lot of our "far away" kin lived in places like Pittsburgh and Harrisburg. In those days "close" relatives were down the block, across the street, or up the alley, but absolutely no farther than twenty miles away, placing them, therefore, either smack in the middle of downtown Huntingdon, or at the northern edge of Altoona. It definitely made them "Sunday dinner eligible" kin. No part of any town in those days was known as *urban* or *suburban.* Either you were downtown or on the edge of town. Sometimes, if you were directing a complete stranger, you could pretend to be Rand McNally and, maybe, refer to certain local areas as "Brewery Hill", or "the laundry field", or "out around Reservoir Park." But you'd have been laughed out of town if your young peers had heard you say something like: "Oh yea, the Smith's, they live out there by Washington

School, *in the suburbs*." Furthermore, if you said to a stranger that the Smith's lived *in the suburbs,* just past the school, on a *cul de sac,* well, forget your happy childhood! Right then you'd have been marked for life, with another notch on your hide for still being the town smart ass, and summarily accused of plotting to undermine local authorities by secretly studying French municipality theory on the side, i.e., "on the side" meaning spare time that was to be prioritized for fine tuning any innate skills you possessed, such as throwing "skippers" across the paper mill creek. People today don't call it "spare time." It's now "quality time"—a phrase that makes me almost throw up. Such "phraseology" erupts from kids spending too much *spare time* absorbing the sounds of *yuppy* parents. And as far as throwing stuff across that stinking, mucky creek, back then that *was* a top priority, regardless of other folk's opinions to the contrary, since our arch enemy Ralphie Franks and his goons were usually on the other side throwing stuff back at us. And who ever heard of a *cul de sac*, or even knew what the hell one looked like, or how to use it? As far as we ever knew, *cul de sacs* were unnamed and "uninvented." If ever asked, we'd have kindly pointed that stranger friend to "the place across from the pile of garbage at the end of the alley," or "down there where the sewer overflows by the side of the road and goes into the woods." And guess what? We'd have never known we were describing *cul de sacs* or any other exotic French contraption. If it wasn't part of the Saturday matinee at the El Patio (Old Potato), then it was strictly foreign intrigue, unworthy of consideration by us juvenile "introspective isolationists." But enough already with the French theory and other "mundanities" of childhood. . . . Back to the ancestors.

Although Dad claimed some of his folks to be borderline notables . . . I don't remember any. The ones we knew up close and personal were mostly blue collar. With the men folk I do recall never being able to picture them spiffed up on a Friday or Saturday night as they headed to the Moose, or Legion, or Fifty Piper's. The true wonder is in remembering the unique way in which they returned from those places. At that late hour they were totally spiffless and a living, breathing testimonial to the indestructibility of the human anatomy, having endlessly defied our precisely calculated odds that they would never return at all. Their homecoming rituals almost recalled casualties returning from the front (God bless'em), or recreation of the last Firemen's Convention (God bless them, too). Almost every week-end night they reprised their roles to perfection.

Grandpa was typical. He was the comic relief to Grandma's rock of granite. He was Pennsylvania Railroad and Loyal Order of the Moose. She was Lutheran Church and card carrying W.C.T.U., staunch and staid (the W.C.T.U. hierarchy hated Grandpa's suggested membership strategies: ". . . a couple o'drinks an' free lunch at the parsonage'll clear evr'y damn bar in town."). Grandpa was liked and respected by his co-workers and peers. But his normal "don't give a damn" attitude around town often conjured up dire outcomes in Grandma's mind . . . things like going to hell . . . or worse: imagined future reprisals from Lutheran lady friends and other woeful beings who might possibly uncover her sin of harboring a godless degenerate on her premises. Grandpa, known to all as Will, daily traveled the Middle Division between Altoona and Harrisburg at the controls of his trusty old Pennsy K4 steam locomotive. I still remember days in 1939 standing in our back yard, waving across the Juniata Creek, as a huge, black, smoking monster barreled through the morning mist, hugging the rails as it gathered speed roaring out of town, heading east with whistle blowing and engineer—red bandana flapping—waving back to an anxious six year old boy . . . a lad bursting with unlimited pride and delight at the fleeting recognition from a real, live steam locomotive engineer—his own real, live grandfather.

Grandpa retired at the end of that year. In two more years World War II would start. During that short period, as I look back, Grandpa probably was often at loose ends. My parents were active in Masonic functions in those years. When they were away Grandma always stayed at the house with us kids. She was great to have around. She possessed ESP. Nobody had a name for ESP then. Grandma didn't even know she had it. It came in handy for her, though. Her technique for watching grandchildren was at all times to keep one eye on us and the other eye on the front or back door. If we were on the porch, the end of the block was never out of her sight. Although Grandma didn't know her own powers, one thing she knew for sure:

At any time Grandpa would be leaving the Moose—condition unknown, course uncertain—well fortified by his booze *du jour* and heavy laden with sodas, sandwiches and pocketfuls of coin. His goal at all times was: divert the enemy (Grandma), commandeer the house atop "Brewery Hill" and rescue the minds of three unwitting kids who, in his everlasting opinion, were under a constant, fierce attack by an unending supply of grandmotherly good intentions. If we were playing outside, Grandma could see Grandpa's lurch on the horizon. She was quicker than a Navy Seal getting us inside and behind locked doors. If we were inside, she simply locked the doors. She kept a huge, besom broom handy—courtesy of the local Lions Club—to fend off occasional, spirited "Grandpa surprise attacks." One summer evening, Grandma—a petite woman—was in the back watering the garden. Out of nowhere, like Stanley finding Dr. Livingstone in darkest Africa, Grandpa fell flat against the front screen door. With darting eyes he saw that the coast was clear. Before we kids could've said, "Grandpa, . . . I presume," he pushed through the door in a blaze of satisfaction and confidently rushed to our "aid" in the living room. His scant moment of glory was short lived as, seemingly from nowhere, Grandma arose out of the dust—with God at her side and broom in her hand—to brow beat Grandpa out of the house, across the front porch and onto the sidewalk, as finally, in full retreat, he shuffled despondently down 12th Street, moving eventually out of sight. He probably tasted straw for days after that particular foray into uncharted territory. Grandpa's visits were always forcibly short—but never quite that short. In his altered state, he was easily discouraged by Grandma's resolve and usually just left his coins and stash of goodies on the porch and stomped away into the twilight, foiled again by Grandma Zorro and her magic Lions Club broom. Grandma's explanation on these entertaining episodes was always the same. "You're grandfather's sick, children. It's God's curse." We never questioned her wisdom, except to note in later years that Grandpa's constant poor health in those days was surely prosperous for us kids in a Depression year. In today's society Grandpa would've been dead meat for his antics. Consider: walking under the influence (WUI), public nuisance, jay walking, harassment, child abuse, spousal abuse, attempted break-in, littering, reckless endangerment (his own), suspicion of burglary and leaving the scene of a crime.

Grandma's only sin was her cooking. She was a good cook. But bad cooking was Grandpa's idea of good eating. Grandma obliged him. His indelicate eating habit was legendary. Had Grandpa's excesses been common to humans during biblical times, Methuselah could have just as likely been named poster boy for pre-mature death syndrome. A "grandpa" typical breakfast consisted of six eggs fried in lard, half-a-pound of liver pudding floating in about three quarts of grease, roughly two pounds of potatoes sliced and fried in lard, about four pieces of stale bread spread with half-an-inch of, you got it, more lard, all washed down with unlimited cups of three-day old, black coffee from a pot that hadn't been cleaned since John Alden spoke for himself. As he ate, beads of sweaty grease rolled down Grandpa's jowls. In the final stages of the meal, he usually commenced a grand scheme to meticulously swab all the leftover "sludge" from his plate and sop any remaining dregs from his heavily stained coffee cup. With grave solemnity, while holding his last piece of stale bread in hand—a gesture truly deserving a global moment of silent prayer—he would execute a grand routine of culinary mop-up that made Holy Communion look like a pagan ritual. Sometimes, then, afterward he would stand and declare, "Thank God, I don't use salt . . . they say it's a killer."

After breakfast he went to his chair for his pipe and morning paper. Between the kitchen and living room, Grandma endured more torture as Grandpa belted out the mangled, half-remembered, ungodly lyrics to some obscure railroader's chantey. The tune, a regrettable, best-left-forgotten ancient melody, was delivered in a throaty bass voice that resonated close to twenty-five octaves off-key. He was the great Irish tenor, John McCormack, "run amuck." The rest of his day—between meals, that is—consisted of taking turns at his tobacco pouch, several pipes and half a dozen cigars. For a nightcap, he sometimes nipped from a secret stash of booze hidden somewhere in Grandma's kitchen. He seldom drank at home. Once, in 1950 when we lived in Harrisburg, Grandpa came to visit. He enlisted my brother, Frank, as his "trusty pathfinder" and they both set out to discover a local tavern. Frank ordered a soft drink. Frank later recalled that while he was sipping root beer, Grandpa downed four double shots of blended whiskey, chased them on the side with a modest pitcher of domestic lager, ate a half dozen pickled eggs from the "free lunch," and then proceeded to advise the pub owner on the merits of volume buying so to be ready for his next visit to the city. Grandpa died suddenly in 1952 at age seventy-eight, a generous span of years for those days. He wasn't a lush or a bum. He was a good father and provider. He was a gentleman. He was Grandpa.

Grandma's name was Amanda. After her Will died, she went back to good cooking and healthy eating. Television was just new then. Grandma became infatuated with "professional wrestling." She never missed a performance . . . a reminder of her broom wielding days of old, no doubt. In the 1960s she identified with shows like *I Love Lucy* and Jackie Gleason's *Honeymooners*; programs, I am sure, that would still have earned critical acclaim had they been otherwise known as *The Will and Amanda Show*. Grandma lived to be ninety-six.

I never knew my mother's parents. But she had boat loads of other relatives hanging around for years. In my hometown in 1939 there were tons of them. At a family reunion in 1980 there were about eighty, or so, remaining from the original issue. Funny thing about that reunion . . . I hardly knew them in '39, and yet, forty odd years later, some were still strangers. It's a nice feature with reunions. If you keep them far enough apart—and everyone stays healthy—you get two "strange" sets of relatives for the price of one. Mother's family came from Germany. She had about fifteen aunts and uncles on her mother's side and, maybe, eight or nine more on her father's side.

Mother's brother, Tom, was my favorite of the maternal ancestors. Uncle Tom left our town shortly after World War I and became a successful businessman in the Midwest. Most summers he returned to Tylertown to visit family and look up old friends. During a summer visit in 1947, shortly after a "whirlwind tour" of the downtown Tylertown saloons, Uncle Tom "innocently" showed up late for dinner with one of Mother's old childhood admirers. Since their earlier years, as I later learned, this particular beau, Pug Lytle by name, had digressed from the high ground as one of Tylertown's socially credentialed thoroughbreds, to now wear the mantle of "prominent, low-level town drunk" (albeit a friendly and fuzzy one) who was, at that moment, seated across from me at our dinner table, with head bobbing and weaving, about to tip over his chair as he strained for a look into the kitchen where my Uncle Tom was on the receiving end of a royal ass chewing by my usually passive mother. Uncle Tom was feeling no pain. Pug Lytle felt even less. Mother was just about mad enough to say "hell's bells"—her strongest profanity in my memory. After the initial excitement subsided, Mother kicked it into afterburner mode. There would be no "blue plate special" that day. She served and cleared the meal with bursts of speed and energy surpassed only years later when NASA started launching missiles into space. Pug was silent throughout. Despite Mother's murderous stare, Uncle Tom kept blurting out conversational tidbits—still playing the "innocent"—trying to resurrect childhood memories, seemingly to make drunken table talk sound like one of ex-President Roosevelt's famous "fireside chats." Pug didn't, or couldn't, react. Either he was too drunk, or my mother's presence there simply overwhelmed him—probably a little of both. Mother was a typical housewife of the times. She had great poise and class. Today they would call her straight-laced and out of touch; in that era they called it being a lady. At that time I was a young teenager. From the conversation that day, however, I guessed that Pug had a history of intimidation by Mother's somewhat stoic bearing. Later, at the front door, he struggled to thank her for the meal. There were tears down his cheeks as he searched for just the right words. He mumbled in a drunken brogue. "I a'ways thought o' you and a'ways r'member you an' yer fam'ly from the ole' days." He stared at her for an eternity and struggled for composure. When he again spoke it came from deep within him. Mother, I think, was feeling both complimented and totally embarrassed until he grasped her hand in both of his and cried, "Cora, yer still a god'dam jewel!" After that, Mother was just embarrassed.

Looking back, those years were hard working, fun loving times by a God fearing group, mostly of German descent. When I dwell on our lives today, it's truly sorrowful to consider that something has since slipped away. Computer wizards, these days, solve everything by "interfacing." Where did that word come from anyway? And what the hell does it really mean? How about a "planet earth cultural interface"? Take every culture . . . the old and the new . . . all backgrounds, all beliefs. Interface puritanical with satanical—today's smash-mouth/trash-mouth culture—and maybe level the playing field just a bit. Perhaps the old-timers will stand and say, "We had the same right to be crude and rude and uncaring, as self-centered as you. . . . But we did care and it gave us pride and a way of life we thought would never pass. . . . We didn't have to give a damn, either, about family, or church, or our country's flag. . . . But we did. Nothing but conscience and the right stuff ever kept us from vilifying God's name in schools and public places. . . . Whose God is it, anyway—yours, mine, ours? Who has the right to choose? So what if God is a he or a she, or black or white or gray or purple, or Christian, Jew, Muslim or Harry Potter, or an ex-senator from South Carolina? Get over it! . . . We honor one God; and, like it or not, there only *is* one God. God's gift is life. As part of His gift, we . . . all of us . . . own the privilege to live and the potential to do. It's not about burning buildings, flags and books, or heaving dung at icons for the precious little attention you never got from rotten parents who always treated you like a rock. It's about faith and good works, stupid! . . . How simple can it be?"

In my youth there was nothing to stop our elders from the same idiocy that today passes for equality, morality and justice. Nothing possibly except an ingrained personal honor system and, maybe, for the fact that it never entered their minds. They had their problems, too. We still have problems. Once, we were capable of everything . . . and did nothing. Today, we do nothing . . . and have everything. The best to hope, I think, is that life is seasonal—that man's passion and power can turn and return. In the old days we thought of ourselves as Americans—not German Americans, Asian Americans, Italian Americans, Irish Americans, African Americans or Lower Slobovian Americans. Ours was the American way . . . an American heritage . . . a proud heritage. We're still proud . . . proud Americans. Still . . . how did we get to here from there? How do we get back?

Over the long haul from youth until now we have always been free to follow, or stray from, the chosen path of our ancestors. The lesson taught was that the ability "to do" belonged to anybody at anytime "to do it"—in the best ways that we knew. After all, we had "done it" to a depression. We had "done it" to unholy upstarts in a fight called World War II. We continued "doing it" by putting postwar America on top again through prolific achievement in every avenue of daily life. Somewhere we stopped, or something else started. We rested too long on our oars. As a nation we got long on potential and short on motivation.

My father wrote some music before he died. The title says it all for me. He called the piece "Nobody Thought To Ask Me." It was meant for a nostalgic/comedic music hall, or vaudeville, setting. From the few scribbled notes that he left, the lyrics were to suggest a life of lost potential and unfinished business. His stained, precisely penned sheet music was found among private papers. He never finished the lyrics. Sadly, I suppose, nobody thought to ask him. Nobody asked me, either; but my lyrics say this:

> "I could have found the Lost Chord in a day,
> I made the first Frisbee an' threw it away,
> Take that telescope Hubble, I'd have made it a double,
> But nobody thought to ask me.
>
> I recall the Depression, the country went under,
> It was simple to think up a cure for that blunder,
> And the hoop they called hoola,
> Would've rolled me in moola,
> But nobody thought to ask me.
>
> We might have been sweethearts, the perfect pair,
> Partners for life, but who was to care,
> That while I was somewhere in worlds of my own,
> You simply grew tired of being alone,
> And I never thought to ask you."

Chapter Two

Retirement

Retirement gives me reflection . . . for instance: How in the hell did I get so old so fast? Death knell oracles reveal: At the moment of death, life passes in review. Retirement gives me a sense of that moment. Right now, if I had my d'ruthers, I'd be shouting the line Anita O'Day was singing with Gene Krupa's band in 1941: ". . . just let me off uptown."

My life, and life for most of my generation, was defined by events of the late 1930s and 1940s. It was about the Great Depression, World War II and the music and affairs that accompanied that memorable era. Most of us detest the torturous misfortunes of those years. None of us forget the endurance.

I catch myself lately, almost in mental relapse, sorting out the early memories. Awareness of conscious life and surroundings began around 1937. My younger brother had just been born, capping my parents modest family at three boys. I had no sense of it then, but life in the 1930s was desperate for young folks like my parents.

The world was in economic depression. Even the *experts* hadn't a clue as to how, or why, mankind had achieved that pickle, and little, if any, sense as to when we would finally get over it. President Franklin D. Roosevelt (FDR) got the credit. But it took a world war to really do the trick. In those early years the simple things in a child's life were seldom momentous. Now, however, I know that "simple things" didn't just happen. Through those hard times, typical parents of typical families sacrificed and anguished as they struggled to make life's daily existence natural and easy flowing. Thinking of my parents and others during those years I recall the opening line of Rudyard Kipling's "If—," "If you can keep your head when all about you are losing theirs and blaming you; . . . ."

From memory I distinctly recall that we ate like royalty. Granted, in 1939 I wasn't exactly into comparative lifestyle analysis; but who can say otherwise. The milk was wholesome . . . just add water to the dry, white powder. There was a lot of potato soup, most times watery, some times creamy. It was nourishing. A common supper was bread soup—bread, milk and sugar, sometimes with coffee added for the adults. Oatmeal was big at breakfast since, as my mother assured, "it sticks to your ribs." It also stuck to the wall if you were into paper hanging, and could've doubled as putty or caulk for custom-made window installation. Eggs were plentiful—also, sometimes powdered. Bread and assorted baked goods was plentiful since Mother's brother, John, owned the local bakery. Sunday dinner was the big meal. Usually we had chicken or veal—both, oddly enough, relatively cheap in those years—followed by "scratch" cake and ice cream topped with any available scrumptious ingredients Mother could put together. Maybe there was a Great Depression out there. At the time, you couldn't prove it by me.

In 1939, at age six, I was permitted to have a birthday party. Mother invited about ten of my school friends from first grade. The invitations were homemade, a single page cut from construction paper. Recently, I found one of them in an old scrapbook. Mother had printed the required information in the center of the card. Several doo-dads had been crayoned around the border—no doubt, by yours truly. In the way of a post script Mother had allowed me a personal touch at the bottom. In penciled capital letters my P.S.

read:

WE ARE HAVING REAL MILK.

Hoboes were common throughout the Depression. On most days it was normal for Mother to answer a knock at the back door and be met face-to-face by some dingy "man of the road"—down on his luck—looking for a handout to keep him going until his next *scheduled* meal. Mother fixed them sandwiches, usually from leftovers on hand, then, typically, added a couple hard boiled eggs, a cookie and a cup of water or black coffee. Although doors were seldom locked in those days, hoboes always came to our kitchen entrance and politely knocked. Gentlemen of the road—professional tramps—are a nostalgic piece of history and have not completely vanished. Hobo camps, or jungles, are still around. Hoboism, for many, is a celebration of life, a better way of life.

In our present culture—and for good reason—seeing dirty, sleazy strangers constantly rapping at back doors would cause panic in the neighborhood. First instincts would propel a prudent man straight to his gun rack with a definite plan to blow the trespasser away. In most situations, unfortunately, attack probably would be the right move. Since the mid-1960s, the odds steadily increased that any suspicious character skulking about your property was likely after your money and/or your life. The stark leniency in our laws since then has often meant a free pass to many whackos who should've already walked death row or been locked up for life.

For Americans, the real war started on December 7, 1941, when the Japanese imperial forces attacked Pearl Harbor. Our family moved around a lot after that. Dad worked for the Pennsylvania Railroad. It seemed that we moved every year. Then in 1947 we happily returned to Tylertown and our roots. During our years on the road we virtually lived out of storage crates. Because of his erratic work schedule, Dad missed most scheduled meals with the family. As a result, he was often seen eating at the oddest hours, day or night, and became somewhat of a fixture in Mother's kitchen. Through it all, while oblivious to our curious stares, Dad developed uncommon skills at eating over the sink. In the evening, particularly, standing there, slightly stooped, he learned to balance and devour as much as a six-course spread, wash and dry his dishes, and get to the radio for Lowell Thomas and the news in about thirty minutes. His body was so conditioned that on nights when he could be home to sit and eat with the family he often got leg cramps. Wherever we lived during World War II, in each city the sense of patriotism and priority toward the war effort was constant. Those days personalized a snapshot in time . . . a time so compelling to our future appreciation and understanding of being an American. Over sixteen million Americans served the cause. The whole country was a team pulling for the cause of democracy and freedom. Although I was only a grade school student, my strongest feelings remain forever back in those distant years. In 1942, while living in Wilkes-Barre, PA, a few of us nine-year old neighborhood kids heard rumors concerning plans to form a "junior cadet corp" in each branch of the service to help fight the war on the homefront. At once, we all headed out to the local recruiting offices to sign up. Naturally, as we soon learned, it was only a rumor. We were embarrassed to be so gullible. A strange thing, though,—strange, we thought at the time—no one ever laughed at us, or razzed us for being stupid little kids. And it felt pretty damned good, too, as we "veterans" marched back home, secretly relieved, I think, that we'd still be sleeping home in our own beds at night—at least for the foreseeable future. An organization that *was* real, however, never made it to our neighborhood. (Either that, or I flunked my physical and was classified 4F.) Taking a cue from the comic strip character Little Orphan Annie, many children across the country joined a group called Junior Commandos, which was modeled after the Army, with captains, majors and colonels. These kids signed up for the duration. They collected scrap metal, as well as cooking fats and greases, and performed other homefront war duties—including war games—as required. Excess fat and grease yielded glycerin for high explosives. Our neighborhood schools missed out on the Junior Commandos. We performed scrap drives without the formal "chain of command" and, by all accounts, did credibly well. Every class pitched in as we scavenged the neighborhoods, creeks and dumps around town with wagons and burlap sacks looking for old tires and anything made out of metal. Once a week we took our pennies and nickels to school and bought War Saving Stamps. Any kid lucky enough to be getting a weekly allowance in those days, usually spent it on stamps. One stamp cost a dime. Each $18.75 worth of stamps (187 stamps plus a nickel) was traded for a twenty-five dollar War Bond. Savings stamps and bonds were sold everywhere, including the lobby of all movie theaters. War bond rallies were common. Rationing affected every family in those days. Food, clothing, tires and fuel were all in short supply. Every town had a Rationing Board to control availability according to need, with a combination of points and stamps. The most heartrending scenes of the period, however, occurred daily at railroad depots across the nation. To the tunes of Sousa and George M. Cohan, innocent lads with great, confidant smiles, paraded through downtown, USA, to the train stations where they were inevitably torn from the arms of sobbing mothers, wives and sweethearts and hustled onto troop trains that carried them off to training bases and then usually to the war zones, either in Europe or the Pacific. With a flavor of turbulent patriotism and poignancy, exposure to those unreal moments, once experienced, stays with you forever. So many of them never returned.

Death, and notification of death, was especially cruel, leaving stark, angry thoughts on the air. For the survivors of ill-fated loved ones, the horror of reading *killed or missing in action* from an innocuous telegram, so impersonally rendered, at least, gave finality to morbid fears of receiving no report at all. The *moment* of the message, however, would forever haunt their existence. Through all the coming years, that gruesome instant would hang on. Anniversaries, especially, would evoke bittersweet anguish of mixed sorrow and joy, as the personal pain of some impersonal, faraway foreign war had to be re-visited again and again, year after year. The fact of *life altering words,* sealed inside an envelope for delivery on a grim, drear night and read beneath the insipid gaze of a Western Union boy—himself, barely able enough for the two-wheeler bike he rode—was an ordeal for the ages. A simple, commemorative flag of death—gold star on white—would be displayed always from a mother's, or widow's, front window, telling the world of the unending grief inside. And, finally, mercifully, the grieved would find a bright, new day, but never a holiday from the adornment of stone and wreath—an endless graveyard display—that would ordain life's greatest sorrow in perpetuity. There were happy moments: V-mail, Rosie the Riveter, V-E Day, V-J Day and dancing in the street to Glenn Miller's "G.I. Jive" and "American Patrol." I feel sorry for kids today. They will never grow up the way we did. The good and bad from those war years collectively forged our souls into a noble citizenry, patriotic Americans all.

There is a boom today. Tons of books, movies and TV specials are being produced about the last sixty years. But everything done is in the image of today. Nothing rings true. The film *Pearl Harbor* is the latest corrupter of history (unless folks were alive on Sunday, December 7, 1941—and at least six years old—they can't begin to know the meaning of Pearl Harbor. Unless they were there and returned alive, they will never understand Pearl Harbor).

Americans fought and died in five wars during the twentieth century. After the two world wars, in 1950 the Korean War started. Korea was the forgotten war. Originally, it was called a *police action* and finally the Korean Conflict, even though 1.5 million Americans served and 54,000 died. The inscription on the Korean War Memorial in Washington, DC, states that "Freedom is not free." The Vietnam War was the longest American military action (eight years) from 1965 to 1973. Vietnam was a politician's war. Unfortunately, our politicians deferred, leaving the fighting and dying to the American troops. 47,000 Americans died. The Persian Gulf War (Desert Storm) was the efficient conflict, lasting about three months and deploying the largest group of air and ground forces since World War II. Since the end of Desert Storm and, now, the beginning of a new barbaric threat to civilization, I often wonder about the future of our great nation. When is God going to throw in the towel? It sometimes feels that—like the Roman Empire—the days of the American *empire* are numbered. We have since surfaced from an eight year legacy of "blame and shame." The trinity of recent times has been whoremongering, pathological lying and abusing power. Many people demanded: "Where was the outrage?" There never was much of a response. *While a nation slept . . . and so on, . . . and so on.*

Several years ago, during our national Memorial Day celebration televised from Washington, DC, not one civilian member of the Clinton administration was on camera. I don't say that they were absent. They just weren't conspicuous by their presence. To paraphrase an earlier statement of Vice-President Al Gore who, on the occasion of his donning a mantle of stupidity as explanation for his comatose attendance at a controversial fund raising debacle, said: "I made several trips to the bathroom. Possibly I missed that." That's possibly the answer, then. They all were in the bathroom. Two nights earlier on C-Span, the talented Robin Williams brought down the house during a Democratic Party tribute to President Clinton. It was bitter partisan politics and profanity at its raunchiest, hitting the airways in prime time. Several days before, the Supreme Court had overturned the Telecommunication Act of 1996 in favor of Playboy Enterprises by relaxing the censorship laws on sexually explicit TV. This now allowed us to view unscrambled sex all day long instead of just at night after the kiddies have been tucked away. Whoopee! Our constitutional rights were saved once more. Also, it made for a nice little "Lucky Strike extra" for the guys getting off third shift. Morning TV could now be a toss up between *Sesame Street* and *Debbie Does' The Dallas Cowboys*. Chalk up another concession to the liberal law of the land.

The rate of proliferation of pornography into our daily lives was record breaking and unprecedented during the Clinton Administration. One of my recently adopted goals in life is to live long enough to hear real comedy again—comedy that entertains with timing, presentation and funny situations . . . not from some rambling diatribe connected by fifty-five obscenities describing every private body part in Gray's Anatomy—including the *coccyx* because it sounds dirty; or where religious connotations are taboo except in mocking or taking of a name in vain (I hate to sound preachy about it 'cause I sure as hell ain't no saint, but it's what I believe). The entertainment world has always been chock full of talent. Talent spawns influence and influence affects people and lifestyles. Where are the role models that someday will emulate the likes of Red Skelton, Bill Cosby and Dick Van Dyke? As for me, in the present, where we have "free-speech, free-everything Hollywood zealots with a message," I say, shoot the messenger. To paraphrase the Korean War Memorial inscription, "Free speech is not free, either." Let's hope this nation of ours can re-group in the face of our new crisis of terrorism and become the American Empire again.

Consider the common place things and events of today versus thirty years ago and beyond. Frivolous lawsuits alone are enough to drive you bananas. A while back a group of high school seniors, including one of their teachers, were moved to impart a unique message to future generations. While shooting their class picture for the high school yearbook, they gave the finger to the camera when the photographer said "smile." When school officials took a dim view of the event, both students and parents were distraught and offended. The picture and yearbook were re-done without the finger waving scholars. Disciplinary action was taken by the school board. Lawsuits by parents will certainly be forthcoming since the ACLU is now involved. There are good things too. Giant steps have led to unbelievable medical advancements. Today most people have some form of paid medical insurance. On the other hand, our society is a "gimmee" group when it comes to doctor's and hospitalization. Everything is taken for granted. Not so long ago there were *family* doctors. Often they treated patients at home (an archaic event known as a *house call*). On many visits you paid cash on the spot. Cash-on-the-spot, however, didn't mean a second mortgage on the house. Once upon a time, doctors did have reasonable rates. But then, doctors weren't faced with huge malpractice insurance premiums. And that brings us back to frivolous lawsuits, etc., etc., *ad nauseam*. Another good thing: Yesterday we didn't know a headache from a brain tumor. On the other hand, according to the latest studies, these days everything we do or eat eventually causes some fatal disease in mice and, therefore, in humans. If you're doing or eating something with no assigned malady as yet, don't give up. Your day will come—either in the courts or in the morgue. Years ago we didn't have a million research teams working on things like the medicinal benefits of powdered gnat testicles, or why one drink a day is just dandy, while two or more will lead you through Alcoholics Unanimous on the way to the top of the scrap heap of life. The big issues of yesterday for teenagers were alcohol and sex. They are still key issues . . . with one more added: drugs.

There is a critical discrepancy between the generations of yesterday and today. How did it occur? Will it ever be resolved? A few generations ago we went on a problem solving mission. Many folks think that it worked. We took prayer and any reference to God out of school. Then we became concerned that, as parents, we were abusing our children. We followed the advice of lovable, old Doc Spock—who was to child psychology as I am to beet farming—and we stopped spanking them. At the same time we decided against our school teachers bruising their little psyches, too. That could bring on a lawsuit or two. Oh, yea! And let's get rid of those nasty back alley butchers and all those dirty, illegal abortions. Let's clean up our act and get nice new, sterile clinics for the girls. Give'em the best that money can buy. First thing, though, we have to change the law and make it legal. Explaining right from wrong doesn't address the problem anymore since we don't recognize that school of thought these days. And teaching abstinence won't help because they'll just go out and do it anyway, just to spite us. There is one solution, though. Let's show some compassion and take the pressure off of the boys. We'll give them condoms at school. And to be fair, let's make them available to the girls, too. That way we cover all the bases. We can work the added cost into the school lunch budget. Now we're cooking! Our problems are fading like boomerangs into the wind. Stand back! You ain't seen nuthin' yet! Let's stop being so picky with our legislators. The economy's good. We have jobs, money and security. Who cares what the hell they do in private, or even what they tell us they do in private, or don't do, for that matter? Turn the other cheek. Besides, everyone does it. And let's stop being so damn silly. Why can't First Amendment rights be more compatible to the new sophistication and enlightenment of our citizenry? *Screw the geezers! They're just gonna' have to learn appreciation of good literature.* (Example: You select a book at random. Despite an innocuous title—*Humpty Dumpty Had A Great Fall*—you remember that the critics raved. You begin reading. At once, you're into rape, incest, extra marital hanky panky, divorce, gratuitous sex, lesbianism, sadism, Satanism, robbery, embezzlement and murder, not to mention language that would turn your shorts blue. On top of all this, Humpty Dumpty's *great fall* is really erectile dysfunction. Throwing the book aside, you walk away wondering if page two might have been better.) Also, don't get hung up on pornography laws—child, adult or otherwise. Simply preach that *"evil is in the eye of the beholder."* We should start, also, registration of firearms. That way we can find them faster when confiscatory policy becomes law. In the past, other countries have done it with great success. Look at them now. . . . Say, what? . . . Nazi Germany? . . Who the hell were they? . . . One more thing: Our prisons are overcrowded . . . unfit for human habitation. The prisoners—poor souls— already have paid so dearly for simply minor infractions. Let'em go! What's the big deal over rape and armed robbery if no one gets hurt? . . . It's our way of life today—hardly worth a slap on the wrist. . . . Everybody does it. While we're at it let's get rid of this business they call *capital punishment*. It's simply too brutal. And we know that in their "heart of hearts" the poor dears would never even swat a fly.

One of my favorite actors from the old days in movies was George Tobias. In the World War II flick *Air Force*, George played the part of Corporal Weinberg, a B-17 gunner fighting Japs in the Pacific. Corporal Weinberg's comment on his dislike of California parallels my own view of traveling the bumpy road to *senior citizenry* and retirement: "The sun shines and nothing ever happens, and before you know it you're sixty years old."

Chapter Three

Foolin' Around

"Fooling around" means whatever you want it to mean. In my rendering it applies to boys and girls and relationships. Neither type nor degree of heat in a particular relationship has changed in the last sixty years. Relationships can be Platonic, emotional or physical, or just emotional and physical. Relationship partners can be best friends, just friends, puppy loves, unmarried, engaged, married, extra-marital, divorced, widowed or dead. The major difference in relationships between 1935 and the year 2000 and beyond is the timeline of change in social attitudes toward males and females going together, or seeing each other, or dating, or going steady, or making out, or making it, or getting it on, or going all the way, or shacking up, or sleeping together, or whatever else human pairs can conjure.

Moral laws have become archaic. For one, the idea of conception and birth inside wedlock is grossly passe. Our urges and desires are meant to be vented, regardless of time and place. Man needs and seeks both philosophic and sexual freedom. The puritanical bonds of our ancestors should be discarded. We have become self-imbued by an aura of enlightened sophistication and intelligence. Mankind is rapidly moving toward mystical horizons, but only for the betterment of the species. . . . At least, this is what the sociologists and a lot of other peabrain whackos are preaching.

Here's what the geezers say: What damned hellacious epidemic happened in the last forty years that caused men and women of any age to slither to the level of cats and dogs in the alley? Is nothing sacred or private any more? In our heyday we were no angels, but there sure as hell was a big difference in the shades of right and wrong as we understood it. And if we didn't know, our parents told us. If we still pretended not to know, well, then we were in for some tough love. The point is that our parents communicated. Some young people today think that abstinence is an after dinner drink. Their elders, however, being part of the enlightenment, understand that it's actually an *apres diner liqueur*, and from earlier knowledge, rumored, sometimes, to make the heart grow fonder. No matter if it's abstinence, absinthe or absence, why is it so common anymore that the damned inmates are running the prison? Where did reason ever go? Why such stupidity? At least seniors have an excuse. We can fall back on Doddering's ancient theory of *fractium senilis cogitatum,* which roughly translated means: "all imagination, no memory".

To this very day, at age sixty-five, in a drugstore, I feel uncomfortable walking past the "rubbers" on display for all the world to see, with their lavish colors, sizes, lubricants and various other functions. As a boy, I never imagined the day when someone could simply stroll into a drugstore and buy condoms off the shelf. I still muse that one probably doesn't even need a note from a parent. Consider this scenario:

Mom: Where are you going, son?

Son: Just to the drugstore, Mother. I'm fresh out of condoms and CVS has a great sale . . . two for one this week on Trojans.

Mom: Oh. That's nice.

Dad: Take this coupon, son. For an extra buck it'll get you a gross of manufacturers "seconds." We can split 'em.

Son: Gee, cool, Dad.

Mom: Hurry back, dear. Supper's soon ready. It's your favorite . . . pot roast . . .with apple pie and ice cream for dessert.

In my day "just going for rubbers" was never an option. If you tried, it was like planning for World War III. After forging the note from somebody's parent, we took about fifty years to think about and scope out the "target" from the corner across the street. We absolutely never made our move until the place was empty, about to close, or both. Eventually we crossed the street. In front of the store we tried our best to be nonchalant passers-by, despite pacing the sidewalk like union pickets waiting for our signs to arrive. Upon careful "serious" deliberation, the official "rubber runner" was finally selected (they choose the Pope with less bravado). Although trying to be low-key and avoid attention, we still managed to inundate our "inductee" with a round of spirited rump slaps and last minute instructions—high fives were a thing of the future. The poor, brainwashed sucker was usually new to our crowd and either too dumb or too scared to refuse "an honor not lightly bestowed." After all, every kid knew that acceptance of the condom challenge meant instant fame and immediate recognition as "one of the guys." On cue, our pigeon charged the drugstore entrance with the *esprit' de corps* of lemmings at the white cliffs of Dover. Once inside, however,—and it never failed—the master plan quickly unraveled. Our hero immediately fell prey to some weird, twitchy over-the-shoulder spasm, as if expecting to find parents, teachers, preacher and Sunday school class all gathered for ice cream at the soda fountain while collectively watching his grand moment of stealth. As a result, our now super-cautious "guinea pig" stuffed the note in his pocket and spent about ten minutes walking the aisles of an empty drugstore and sticking out like a sore thumb. Regardless of our precision planning, it was always an exercise in futility. When finally approached by a curious druggist, our failed "inside man" would inevitably feign innocence, ignorance or stupidity and blurt out some dumb remark such as, " . . . jus' checkin' the price of bandages for my sister . . . .," like his sister was Clara Barton and the Red Cross was setting up tents on the edge of town. As I said, it was always in futility, but still completely innocent and high adventure for a bunch of young teenagers to enjoy in later years. We never really expected the "great condom caper" to succeed. Failure closed the book. That way, thankfully, we never had to answer classmates' queries at future reunions: *"Whad'you guys ever do with a gross of rubbers?"* And yes, I liked it that way.

During the forties and fifties, promiscuity, as a practice, was not only hard on the reputation, but also unhealthy. Although much rarer than today, in my era it still wasn't the practice of choice in young people's circles. In modern teen-age and young adult circles, casual sex is essentially synonymous with the innocent, goodnight kiss of yesteryear. Surprisingly, it's probably healthier because of condom use—the sex, not the kiss. Thinking back to age thirteen, I was particularly awkward and shy performing my first goodnight kiss. She was fourteen and, having dated older guys of at least fifteen and sixteen, far more experienced at fooling around. Imagine yourself dating in the year 2001 with the moral mind set of a 1940s high school freshman. You escort your young girlfriend to a movie and then go back to her house for the goodnight ceremonies. On the way to her house you're naively exercising your pucker, anticipating a pleasant kiss to finalize a great evening. Meanwhile, for the last twenty minutes, she's been flexing her vaginal sphincters and considering her options: condom or diaphragm, missionary or spooning position (*it's a first date, better keep it basic with this hayseed*). My mind goes blank trying to imagine how this scene would finally conclude. We used to worry about a honeymoon night and consummating the marriage. Now they "consummate" first dates. Where? There's the bedroom, I guess, if her parents aren't home; or, maybe, even if they are home. Otherwise it's a toss up: on the porch, under the porch, over the garage, in the dog house, the tree house, or up against that giant oak in the back yard. Wherever . . . it paints an interesting panorama of moral change and behavior over a fifty year span. Whatever it isn't, I am not certain; however, *it is* downright dangerous, degrading and poor judgment, regardless of peer pressure.

Kids today come by their actions honestly. We live in a climate, both social and political, where perverse attitudes about the so-called *facts of life* come to us right from the top. Speaking for thousands of males from my era, nothing sounds quite as disgusting to a man as some lovely, pert, dewy-eyed, lass with an outward sense of self-esteem, speaking generally about general things—the price of eggs, maybe—in language so universally foul as to make a bos'un's mate blush. Forget that, as brash young punks decades before, our gutter language could capably foul the air at any bull session. And although words are only words, the same words spoken by a man and a woman can impart different connotations which lead to misunderstandings, then to actions and dangerous reactions. In any era, a woman who commands respect will get respect. The nowadays version of self-esteem is a travesty of far better days. In certain crowds today I believe many women are practically throwaways. Unfortunately, I think, they are what they are because they want to be. As teenagers, at exclusively male gatherings, there was a vicious wise crack about girls that we used to repeat and enjoy. The motto of the four F's went: find 'em, feel 'em, f— 'em and forget 'em. Today, I am sure, the same thought, overlaid with a tad more fluff and fancy, is considered *de rigueur* in more than a few supposedly urbane and cosmopolitan circles.

Years ago, most guys of my acquaintance were self-appointed slobs through the high school years. Since we were all involved in athletics there was even more exclusivity to our "slobovian degeneracy." An early unrighteous locker room game—I'm certain we didn't invent it—was to discover the first name of everybody's sainted mother and then speak foul, sexual innuendoes about these sacred ladies in front of any or all team members available to listen, whether in the shower, on the practice field, or in class. I don't remember who started it, except that the sons of the first mother's names to be sullied beat the hell out of him. Since brute force failed to stop the insults, everybody just joined the fun and became an abuser instead of abusee. A few sensitive types stayed offended, thus allowing their mother's names to be targets of record indignities by the rest of us. In the end every mother's reputation got and gave its fair share of verbal abuse. Most of the lines were funny and fairly inventive— not to be repeated here—as well as gross. It sounds odd now to say, but it was all in fun and in the end we all remained friends. The difference, I think, was that our dirty deeds were mere words and stayed strictly inside a select group. No one crossed the line to go public. And most of us recovered from our animal behavior by the time we reached our early twenties.

Most guys then would have gone all the way with any girl in high school. Some would have propositioned certain teachers. It was a conquest thing. Attitudes are no different today. We were always bragging about getting into so and so's pants. Anyone not bragging about it was either being asked or accused of it. It was almost always a lie (except for the student's mother who discovered a pair of panties—not hers—in the glove compartment of the family Buick. The student called it a prop for some magic he was learning. A better magician would've zapped the underwear sooner, wand or no wand). The thing that made claims of sexual conquest a lie was the way girls were in those days. My impression is that most were virgins. In all but a few heated affairs, the girls called the shots. They decided "yes or no." There was no "pill." Few would have carried a personal diaphragm, discreetly packaged in some little crocheted carrying case. Were diaphragms part of a teen-age girl's birth control arsenal in those days? I don't know if they'd even been invented. I know for a fact that the fear of out-of-wedlock pregnancy and an instant "reputation" was greater than the fear of parents and God. Abortions weren't done, as a rule. There were exceptions—some tragic—all unpleasant and risky. The social stigma associated with capricious sexual activity was a great deterrent for boys and girls to keep their pants on. Some guys carried a single condom in their wallet. Among peers, they'd always pull out the old billfold to expound on the need to be alert for instant action—as if the Promiscuous Babes of America Road Show was in town infiltrating the area with a bevy of beauty queens in heat. We all did our share of bragging. Some guys made a career. Believe me, it was almost all talk. Chances were good, however, that some not talking about it were the ones getting it.

As they still do today, religious fundamentalists used to be everywhere shouting about sexual immorality and how it surely paved the straightest way to hell. With the modern day potential for increased traffic in that Satanic direction, far more preachers are around to scream at us and, naturally, major highway improvements have been necessary. The road to hell isn't just plain old Route 30 anymore. It's not even the Pennsylvania Turnpike (except for the moral toll they say we'll pay to travel there). The *highway to hell* has become Interstate 666, eight lanes one way, *gerade aus*; no pit stops, nothing but green lights all the way to the heated hinges. . . . If today's sexual permissiveness had prevailed in the late forties and early fifties—without resources to control collateral fallout—the disease and destruction inflicted upon mankind from such uninhibited carnal activity would've made the Old Testament plagues seem like a strawberry social. The bible thumpers of old would've been as one voice calling for God to mass produce the spaceships to get us "sinners" off the streets and into hell by morning. But ours was a time of stronger moral and social leadership, helping to slow mankind's eventual descent into the amoral abyss of current days. It didn't just happen. Parents learned it from parents and passed it on. Through it all, though, our girls held the key. They kept us straight. In my opinion, they still hold the key. By their words and deeds they are surely able to extract us from the present day morass of egomaniacal humanity in which we dwell . . . pick up the thread of sanity and do good works . . . look to our ancestors and learn . . . and begin to pass it on again. Finally, on the subject of keys, I know that many folks today call codgers of my leaning: old-fashioned. Or worse: *"If he was in charge of the nunnery he'd have the only key to the chastity belts."* I accept their apologies.

What I know and feel is that my generation grew up in a great time, with great events and great memories to look back on in pride. We remember sad times, too. In retrospect, it may not be fair to condemn past generations for slipping a little. Just forgive and understand it. Standards have changed. Perhaps, so too should judgments where young reputations were ruined and future years affected *vis'-a-vis'* the momentary lapse of not keeping it zipped or buttoned until reaching life's "holy grail"—that intangible plateau of wedded bliss deemed by existing standards as the only legitimate intercourse between man and woman favored in the eyes of God and the State of Pennsylvania.

Thomas "Fats" Waller was a popular pianist and cafe singer in the '30s and '40s. Although not reputed as a paragon of the chaste and wholesome life, Mr. Waller recorded a tune in 1940 called "Until

The Real Thing Comes Along":

"I'd lie for you, I'd cry for you,
I'd tear the stars down from the skies for you,
And if that isn't love it will have to do,
Until the real thing comes along."

The message is probably considered laughable today. As I've said about other things: It's God's gift. Cherish it.

Chapter Four

Music

I come from a musical family. I believe that the "Symphonic Intermezzo" from *Cavalleria Rusticana* by Pietro Mascagni is the greatest single piece of music ever written. My children do not. They insist on a Beethoven Sonata, so long as it's served chilled with sauerkraut and pigs knuckles. It is their esteemed belief that David Allan Coe invented music when he wrote and recorded "Take This Job And Shove It." I was raised in the forties and fifties. They grew up in the seventies and eighties. They say my musical tastes run to fire sirens and howling dogs. They are pop music snobs . . . and totally oblivious to sworn statements (by me) that music today is on a fast track to hell.

In my musical memories, the vision of one particular friend is always with me. I met Frankie Rhoads early on in life. She unearthed my musical senses and traveled on. I never knew her well. Even the spelling of her last name is a guess. It was long ago. She was stereotypical of the '40s era bobbysoxer—a cute, bouncy, gum cracking, saddle-shoe clad, wise guy, female dynamo with excess energy in spades. I first met her in 1945. We lived in Balda'mur (Baltimore), Maryland then. Her given name was Frances. She loved to dance. Her whole family loved to dance. They were always dancing. For all I know, maybe they invented dancing. At this moment they all could still be somewhere dancing. I was twelve in 1945; Frankie was probably fifteen, or even sixteen. She lived on Lyndhurst Avenue with her parents, two older sisters (I think) and a younger brother, Buddy, who was about my age. I remember her sister Bernice as a knockout red head. During those war years the Rhoads household was one giant ball of activity all the time. Dancing and whistling people of all shapes and sizes came and went from their house long into the wee hours (the same action today would bring police, fire and S.W.A.T. teams charging forth; no doubt, called by complaining, musically warped neighbors suffering with enlarged Guy Lombardo gene pools). Nothing ever eased up there. The entire Lyndhurst Avenue bunch was committed to a collective energy level of "intense or higher" for the duration (the *duration* equaled *until the war was over*). They, as well as most others, were into everything: scrap drives, War Bond sales, Victory dances, etc.—anything that raised money for the war effort. Frankie Rhoads will never know of my lifetime admiration toward her, or the change she effected in me from the night we first met. She gave me a reason to remember.

All music is pleasing to the senses except hard rock and rap and whatever other kind of discordant pollutants they're substituting for harmonic artistry these days. The net effect is that after exterminating the various rocks, raps and etceteras, whatever remains is my favorite . . . except for the polka. Polkas are a lonely second on my list even though I really enjoy their liveliness. Polkas are for celebrating. Nothing tops even an average Slovak wedding reception with dancing through the wee hours to the tunes of a lively, rowdy polka band. Eventually, though, it all runs together. Soon every lively polka band sounds exactly like every other lively polka band. Polka music is analogous, I think, to the homely lass with a single breast on her back: not much on looks, but fun at the dance. Music is like writing. If it sounds good, it generally is good. For hundreds of years music has been consistently good, proving, I suppose, that life still holds some constants. From era to era, real diversity happens according to the way new generations are free to present their unique style of music as art or entertainment. Since modern day "presentors" and attendees at musical *soirees* are practically at will to be "themselves"—translated: anything goes, no exceptions—often there's the resultant propensity toward cries of police brutality, constitutional rights violations and any other mayhem the lunatic groupie fringe dares bring to the table. Then along comes some "ordained" master spokesperson for the movement with his or her inevitable, fair and balanced justifying cry: ". . . take yer', like, goddam' hypocket'ry an' shove it, gramps! . . . Ya' had yer' riots in the forties an' all yer', like, 'stoned' crazy bobby sockers, ya' know . . . an' yer 'no talent' Snot'ra punk an' 'is 'swoonin' . . . yea! . . . right! An', like, in thirty-eight an' yer 'higher-than-thou' Goodman goons practic'ly ru'ned Carnegie's Hall . . . with what ya' claimed was like a concert . . . a 'jazz concert', yet, ya' know. . . . Christ-aw-mighty, man . . . an' ya' cheered, like, ever' goddam' stinkin' piece, like ya' was at some lousy friggin' Eye'talian soccer cup match, ya' know. . . . An' then ther' was that crap an' all ya' pulled, an' goddam' bedlam one summer there in forty-something in Times Square, New York, an' all yer confetti an' screwin' an' all the promiscu'tory gang bangin' jus' 'cause one o' yer friggin' wars was over again. So shove it up yer' bloody Windsor, mate, an' nex' time don' be sa' goddam' sanctimonial cocky whenever it comes ta' self-es'pression. Yer livin' in the wrong generation gap, if ya ax' me. We gonna' get it on, too! Jus' r'member: We da cool ones, man . . . Janis . . . the Mamas . . . Jimi . . . da great ones don't nev'ah lose it!"

A while back some enlightened music critics of the day gathered to pick the top one hundred popular songs of the twentieth century. Predictably, only one selection—"Over The Rainbow"—was written prior to 1960. I say predictably because *Wizard of Oz*—the movie source of that magnificent song—was just as likely the only G-rated movie these modern musical *doyens* were force-fed between dirty diapers and puberty—their formative "sixties" years. Returning the favor, "Over The Rainbow" was designated their token "golden oldie" from an otherwise musically deprived childhood. We're left then to *ooh* and *aah* over the ninety nine remaining selections—all good tunes—spanning the years 1960 to 2000. Their "esteemed judiciousness," however, whether critical or musical, leaves a void of some sixty-odd years. A time, possibly, when they considered our national musical appreciation level severely limited to "patriotic" Sousa marches and Scott Joplin "dirty dancing darkie" tunes. Most of today's musical personalities escape me. It's not the forties or fifties so I don't follow closely. Except for styles previously mentioned, most of their music is pleasantly entertaining and I like it. On the other hand, a recent top music award went to some obscene, crappy rapper called Eminem for his *sensitive* interpretation of "music" with titles like: "Just Don't Give A Fuck," "Cum On Everybody" and "Still Don't Give A Fuck." Some critics in praising these "songs" said: "Outstanding and well worth your hard earned dollar." What is so damned outstanding about a celebration of drugs, rape, murder, incest and a generally screwed up life? We should, instead, be spending our hard earned coins figuring how to put this, and other similar, undeveloped embryos in a vat of formaldehyde. With Eminem as the national standard, any idiot "artist" of the day, with half the same standards and a seven word vocabulary, is certain to garner untold fame churning out comparable garbage. And they are doing it. Sadly, much talent has gone to seed.

Each time such bullroar goes public I know that Hoagy is out there somewhere with the rest of the dead composers—Johnny Mercer, Henry Mancini, Irving Berlin, *et al*, doing another 360 degree roll and dying all over again for, maybe, the millionth time. In the forties we had silly, non-sensical tunes of our own—"Mairzy Doats," "Huggin' and Chalkin." But, for sure, our lyrics never came close to the current trash with inferences and statements of raping our mothers and sisters or any other entity out there having the vaguest resemblance to the female anatomy. In 1927 Hoagy Carmichael wrote "Star Dust," very likely the most popular—and most recorded--of all twentieth-century songs (the lyrics were written two years later). It is stunning to realize that in seventy-some years we, as a relatively civilized society, have digressed from Carmichael's genius in the immaculate perception of "Star Dust" and its pure, unaffected elegance—a tenon and mortise of verse and refrain—to the pox of plenty now bandied about—by request, no less—by Marshall Mather (Eminem) and peers. In the forties and fifties a high school dance, or any dance, was not complete without at least one turn around the floor to the instrumental brilliance of Artie Shaw's rendition of "Star Dust." One's dance partner was almost immaterial at such moments. The saying: "Either dance well or quit the ballroom,"[2] never applied here. As dance partners go, the cleaning lady would have been fair game. Timing was critical. It mattered, to instantly abscond to the dance floor with the nearest, available female in the building, get her in your arms and into that first stride-like movement before the needle touched the record and the beginning strains of Billy Butterfield's pure-toned trumpet solo soared out above the crowded floor. These are the little gems of memory that outlast the ages. Nat King Cole later recorded the vocal of "Star Dust," an outstanding version with Gordon Jenkins' Orchestra, and another magic event—akin to ". . . the speech of angels; . . . ."[3] The very mention of "Star Dust," let alone the sound of it, easily defined the entire teenage experience for many a "forties" and "fifties" school boy or girl. By contrast, the "rat trap rap" coming from certain "artists" today—with rap sheet for lyrics and melodies that tin eared mothers would disdain—makes some folks physically ill. Some years back, when musical notes were first physically put to paper, we were more than confident it would result in honest-to-God music. Much of it now is a rhapsody from hell, steadily regurgitated by a few of the current crop of so-called "achieving" phenoms. My kids did the clean version of their stuff at age three months. Then with the modern day version of "performing" groups, something else sticks in my craw: As accomplished artists of the day, these fools that we suffer project a pitiful public *persona*: a clump of stumbling high school drop-out types, in backward ball caps and size fifty-two, raggy, baggy overalls hanging off their skinny asses. Posted to both flanks of this misogynic collection is a dressed down, slick haired doxy making with the "shoot the sher'bert to me Herbert" antics, *ala* the classic pedant style of *canis aquarius agita*— wet dog shedding water. If I suddenly returned from a thirty year coma and heard this din, I'd know I was dead and condemned to hell. Think of being hammered senseless with a tire iron to the beat of "Johnny One Note"—better to seek out the relative calm of your local rock quarry. In the old days we had some great "scat singers"—Ella Fitzgerald, Anita O'Day, King Pleasure, Mel Torme, Louis Armstrong, *ad infinitum.* But don't go there for comparisons to the hip hop, rap crap we outlast today. It ain't even close. Sadly, our nowadays "stars" are laughing all the way to the bank. Maybe they're saving their money.

Most modern lyrics go to garbage. In the 1950 movie, *Young Man With A Horn*, Kirk Douglas and Hoagy Carmichael play characters Rick Martin and Willie "Smoke" Willoughby, a pair of down-in-the-dumps jazz players discussing the sorry state of their musical careers. Rick says, "Hey, Smoke, . . . you know what we ought'ta do? . . . We ought'ta make our own records . . . make'em the way we want'em. . . . Boy! . . . We could make records that'ud really split'em wide open . . . make'em sit up. . . . Do some of the old ones . . . like "Dinah," "Twelfth Street Rag," an' "Louisiana Blu—

"They won't buy'em!" snaps Willoughby.

"Who won't?" asks Rick.

"People!" Smoke explains. "You know who buys records? . . . High school girls. You know why? . . . To learn the words. They only buy the new songs to learn the words. . . . Nobody knows what we're doing except us, the guys that do it. They don't hear us, they just hear the words. You and I could drop dead tomorrow an' nobody'd know the difference."

Probably, it's still true about the "words." Some things never change. Lyrics are funny. Lyrics are catchy. Lyrics are sentimental. Lyrics fill our memory banks with songs. Certain tunes would never be "our song" without those same certain words. But it was never about lyrics. It's about the music. Listen to the music . . . pure music . . . harmony, melody. . . . Nothing has changed except . . . what happened to the music?

Dancing to the big bands is one of civilization's missing links, and a lost art. The songs are around to hear in one form or another. But the bands and the ballrooms and dance halls and clubs are gone. Locally, for me, there was: Johnny Long at the Sunset Ballroom in Carrolltown, PA; Hershey Park and Kay Kyser; Les Brown at the Vogue Terrace around Pittsburgh; Louis Prima at the Valencia Ballroom, York, PA, and the Ephrata American Legion, Ephrata, PA

(Louis called it Eff'rayta). The goodness of those days is gone, sadly lost forever . . . except in memory.

    The war in Europe ended in May of 1945. Japan surrendered later, in September. A lot of the older guys we admired from the old "Balda'mur" neighborhood were in the service. Those guys were our real life heroes. Some came back for a visit that year. Jack Roberts was home in late spring on Marine Corps sick leave after getting shot up in Okinawa. His younger brother Bill came home after Navy boot camp that summer and shipped right out again. And Lou Sleater—I don't remember his service branch—was around for awhile. Lou pitched in the major leagues after the war with the St. Louis Browns. Later he capped off his career with the Milwaukee Braves—the team that lost in a playoff to the Brooklyn Dodgers and the right to a World Series spot against the Yankees in 1956. Patriotism was uncontained throughout our neighborhood during 1944 and 1945. On my personal homefront, Dad had worked himself into middle management with the Pennsylvania Railroad and was involved around the clock with crucial troop train scheduling and movements through the Baltimore/Washington, DC rail corridor. He was under obvious strain during those years. From occasional careful remarks he made to Mother, we sometimes imagined an insiders *feel* for the final military push the country was staging against the Axis jerks in Europe and Japan. Our house was on Clifton Avenue, crossing Lyndhurst to the west. Further west, Clifton ran past Cahill Center, the focal point for all activity in the neighborhood. Most middle to lower class neighborhoods then were semi-tough, but civil. We endured sporadic back-alley fist fights and other miscellaneous hell raising feats. We learned to play baseball, basketball and lacrosse. We never had street gangs out there terrorizing old folks and children. The tough-guy stuff was saved for sports at Cahill. My older brother Frank and I spent entire summers hanging out at the Center. The program there was first-rate, organized under the watchful direction of an energetic, hands-on character named Jim Mulvahill. Mostly we played basketball and baseball. My first baseball "horror stories" came from Cahill. But that's another subject.

    Teen and young adult dances were held at Cahill every Friday and Saturday night. The dances were really open to all ages and comprised our young social existence—I never heard the term "social life" until later, except that there I was, during those years at Cahill, having one. More correctly, to a kid who didn't know a fox trot from animal husbandry, I was about to get a social education. The Friday dance was casual dress (what other kind was there?). A live band was out of the question—any musician able to string two notes together was in the service. All the great music we ever needed, though, was right there at Cahill, provided by a worn out "record player" and stacks of well-grooved records.

At one Friday dance Frankie Rhoads briefly took me under her wing. She and my brother Frank were friends and about the same age. The summer before, Frankie had taught brother Frank the jitterbug. Some called it the Lindy. We always called it the jitterbug. Frankie hated a wallflower. At this particular dance, as usual, I was taking up space at the edge of the dance floor with several of my infantile buddies. We were steeped in our regular clownish ritual of fitting in . . ., publicly dispensing our next-to-nothing gems of wisdom concerning the love lives, personal hygiene quirks, mentality, religious affiliation, clothing, etc., about each and every couple who danced by. From the other end of the hall I spied a fierce looking Frankie Rhoads. I thought nothing of it. She was looking in my general direction. Pausing momentarily, her feet suddenly kicked into double-time and she was on the march toward me. I was clueless as to reasons why and cared less. In a breath, just as the first notes of Woody Herman's "At the Woodchopper's Ball" started, she was in my face. "Let's dance!" she demanded. "I can't dance," I said defensively. "What about a jitterbug?" she insisted. "I don't do that, either." With barely a pause she put it in high gear, "You do now, little brother!" Despite her skinny little arms she was like Amazon Annie as she grabbed me . . . dragged me to the middle of the floor . . . and just like that, in about two seconds, I guess, I was jitterbugging, or rather, we were jitterbugging . . . "choppin" wood with Woody and the Herd. . . . Young ladies, look what I'm doin' now! Frankie had the moves of a shimmey dancer spiked on adrenalin. She screamed against the blare of the music: "Keep your feet moving! . . . No one'll know if you're right or wrong! . . . Or if yer doin' a jitterbug, fast waltz, or slow gavotte!" To the beat of the music—like a boot camp drill sergeant—Frankie kept on shouting her brief, but sage, advice at my ear and never lost a step. It was my one and only indoctrination in the Lindy Hop. For fifty odd years at dances, receptions, parties, whatever, I've continued to just "keep your feet moving," with continued thanks for that simple, four-word command demanded by my one and only, first and last dance instructor . . . Miss Francis Rhoads of Balda'mur, Maryland. Oh, well . . . so much for formal lessons. Frankie left me with a special life long memory: her presence at that one particular Friday dance at Cahill Center in 1945. To paraphrase the show stopping words of the great Jimmy Durante, I say in remembrance, "Goodnight, Frankie Rhoads, where . . .ever you are!"

During those early years of my life . . . as World War II was ending . . . thanks again to Frankie, I was able to became one of the few younger "dance masters" at Cahill. I regularly spent Friday and Saturday nights dancing with some of the greatest looking sixteen and seventeen year-old chicks that a five-cent soda could buy. And the fabulous part was—at least I thought so at the tender age of thirteen—when the dance was over I could simply walk away . . . leave'em at Cahill . . . let'em fend for themselves . . . no strings, no problems, no hard feelings . . . no nothing. And so, after the dance, male bonding with my same dis-jointed pals happily continued. With a few more years on my bones I eventually came to grips with the stupidity of that *no nothing* baloney.

Slow dancing was big then, too. To clarify slow dancing for the "now" generations: It was our version of "making out." Boys and girls faced each other on the dance floor and actually did full frontal body touching while stepping out to the ballads of The Mills Brothers, Helen Forrest, Nat "King" Cole, Perry Como, or whoever. Of course, some older couples at times were a bit more intense. They liked to do something called the Sailors Victory Dance, better known as a "naval engagement without the loss of seamen." Unlike some barely are today . . . we were always fully dressed when we danced.

So much great music and memory emerged from those years. My random thoughts of life then are a thousand-fold:

- Sometime between 1922 and 1952, Clarence Beeks of Cincinnati became King Pleasure, an innovator of jazz singing. His style was somewhere between scat and a style dubbed "vocalese" since he fit the words to the contours of instrumentalists improvisations. Pleasure peaked in 1952 and is principally known for his renditions of "I'm In The Mood For Love," "Black Magic," and "All Of Me."
- The British always seemed to have a feel for a song.
- Ray Noble used a singer named Al Bowlly during the 1930's. He was known as England's "Bing Crosby." He was killed during a 1940 air raid of London.
- My favorite big band was Benny Goodman.
- In 1989 I started looking for a CD of Nat King Cole's album called "Where Did Everyone Go?" The album was produced and released in London in 1963. For ten years I searched every possible source to no avail. In 1999, Amazon.com told me it was being re-released on CD due to popular demand. Little did they know that I was the "popular demander."
- Diane Schuur is a fantastic jazz/scat vocalist.
- It seems inconsistent with his on-stage *persona* that Louis Prima composed the classic swing piece "Sing, Sing, Sing" as well as collaborating on the ballad "A Sunday Kind of Love."
- Art Tatum from Toledo earned a conservatory degree in music. He would play the piano non-stop so long as there was Pabst beer on tap, or in cans, or in bottles or paper cups. . . . Well, you get the idea.
- The Lindy Hop, or jitterbug, was named for Charles Lindburgh.
- In the mid-1930's, swing music rescued the record industry from ruin.
- If places could talk: the Savoy Ballroom in Harlem; Connie's Inn in uptown Manhattan; Roseland Ballroom in midtown Manhattan (Fletcher Henderson played piano there); the Aragon in Chicago and Arcadia in Detroit; the Palomar in LA where Benny Goodman was crowned King of Swing at age 26; the Paramount in Times Square, NYC.
- Edythe Wright was the perfect female vocalist for Tommy Dorsey's band.

- Earl "Fatha" Hines from Pittsburgh and the Crawford Grill on "the hill," right across the Allegheny River from Heinz Hall.
- The three Helen's of jazz: Ward, Forrest and O'Connell.
- Critics of jazz and swing said the music led to sex or thoughts of sex. Weren't we always thinking of sex? A glass of warm milk can do that.
- "Blueberry Hill": renditions by Fats Domino, Louis Armstrong and Gene Autrey. If you're a horse it's Autrey's version by a nose.
- In 1946, Kurt Webster, disc jockey on the Midnight Dancing Party from WBT, Charlotte, NC, revived "Heartaches" by Ted Weems (with whistling by Elmo Tanner). Webster, known as "The Night Mayor" of Charlotte, received a Gold Medal for helping to sell a million copies. Ted Weems had to bring his band out of retirement due to the popularity of the record. As a high school teenager at the time, I regularly awoke late at night, tuned my battered, second-hand radio to WBT on low, and awaited Webster's theme music—Artie Shaw's "Nightmare"— to digest the world's greatest big band sounds far into the wee hours.
- Charlie Parker: alto sax genius and intellectual; heroin addict, dead at age 34 in 1955.
- The end of World War II was the beginning of the end for swing bands.
- Some call Eminem music just "silly songs." We should all pray fervently to Phantasia, the patron saint of passing fancies, that his fancy passes.
- A toast to the great "huckleberry" lyrics of Johnny Mercer.
- A former Marine named Jim Burie used to sing with service groups. For what it's worth, when it came to band singers, Jim would've given Sinatra a run for his money.

During the years 1935 to 1955 we danced to the greatest popular music ever written, with arrangements and bands so outstanding that we'll never know their kind again, at least, to the same degree of artistry and sophistication appreciated by the world wide masses of the time. Those tunes and groups and writers came struggling out of the international chaos of the late 1930s and war ravaged 1940s. There never was, nor ever will be, a musical experience to match it. Sixty and seventy years later it remains as fresh and new and in demand as if yesterday never left us, and today never happened.

Chapter Five

Home Improvement

In 1898 it took sixty-six days to build the palatial Vanderbilt mansion in Hyde Park, NY. Today it takes longer to get a simple building permit for a backyard shed.

I was proud that, over the years, my handyman skills had improved. My wife even noticed, I think. Would she admit it? No way! It was always: "When ya gonna get off yer bum and fix the leak in the toilet?" Or, ". . . this place's been a dump for weeks. . . . pretty soon I'm callin' a real handyman." With the skill and acumen of a professional craftsman, routinely I had completed hundreds of home improvement chores. Thousands of dollars had been saved, I'm sure. Just as routinely she'd search out and show me a bent nail that was hammered crooked ten years ago. As I got better, the wife got bitter. For all of forty-four years I endured such grief. Disgusted and unappreciated, on the very day that I retired from work in the real world I decided to hang up my tools at home.

In the old days (ho hum, here it comes again), after sex and children, the greatest imagined satisfaction about marriage was "owning" a home—mine and the bank's, a little private piece of the rock . . . a mortgaged love nest somewhere in the sticks where, as the song goes, you simply "let the rest of the world go by." It was the traditional way that two young love birds cemented domesticity and a happy, fruitful life together. At first, the road to success and happiness was rough for us. During the lean years of depressions, recessions and various other dips and dents in the national economic curve, when the U.S. dollar wasn't worth a twit—the nation's struggle to stay abreast of the English ha'penny was major economic news—a house in the country, any country, was "to die for," a cherished dream to last for years, *ad infinitum.*

Sometime during 1960, my wife and I found ourselves in Pittsburgh, PA, with a spare three hundred dollars to our joint name, and a burning desire to plunge ourselves into long-term real estate debt. In 1960, with "three hundred cash" and an approved VA loan, you could do that. One afternoon we were summoned to appear at offices in downtown Pittsburgh so to finalize the purchase of our first honest-to-goodness, "vine covered cottage." They called it *settlement.* Now there's a genuine misnomer. In truth, "settlement" was about as soothing as Hurricane Hazel, especially considering that as a novice "real estate tycoon" I was fearful of being left to wallow in the untested waters of financial ruin on my first "big deal." As the buyers, my wife and I were placed on one side of a huge, conference table plastered with stacks of unsigned documents. Across this paper mountain we sat staring at a motley gang of unknowns and other disinterested strangers—presumably a gathering of sellers *et al.* They could've been "Admissions People" from Bedlam Asylum signing up a fresh catch. We'd have never known. They sat in a dumb trance, twiddling. Everyone in the room, save yours truly and wife, had garnered one or more writing tools to twiddle until the proceedings began. Suddenly the process was underway as all hell broke loose. Paper and pen flew asunder like slop at the trough. Obviously my spouse and I had missed the all important starting signal. General turmoil was instantly all around us as we both sat dumbfounded. In unison the "sellers *et al*" were screaming of escrows and titles and prorated taxes and spouting legalese from the

Latin and Greek and, for all I knew, from Elizabeth Barrett Browning's "Sonnets from the Portuguese." "What the hell are we into, now?" I wondered out loud, glancing at my shaken spouse as she appeared to pinch the skin of her right arm, trying, I imagined, to crush the capsule beneath and experience the comforting solace of cyanide. "We can't be in the right place," I mumbled. "This is crazy! . . . All this mayhem for a dump of a six-room 'fixer upper.'" . . . The room was in chaos. A new worry struck me: Possibly, unknowingly, we'd agreed to a package deal and were now buying Three Rivers Stadium along with the house. The entire affair was stupefying, . . . a scene straight from the end of World War II in the Pacific: me and the wife with General McArthur and President Harry Truman, planted on the deck of the battleship Missouri, co-signing terms-of-surrender documents as the Japanese nation capitulated to the world. Perhaps, we'd all exchange pens later.

The net outcome of that agitation was our very first "cottage for two"—that well-known, typical "handyman special"—worth "two grand" on the open market and seventy five thou' in my mind. On moving day, twenty-nine days before the first monthly payment came due, the roof sprung a leak. The next week an old water heater ruptured. The basement was mindful of "ole' man river rollin' along," *sans* William Warfield, baritone. Squirrels were in the attic. . . . Termites were gorging on *haute cuisine* in our tiny hall closet. Bills for the plumber, electrician and exterminator were on the kitchen table. Checks for car repairs from backing into and destroying the garage door, deposits for telephone, gas and electric, etc., etc., etc., right on down the line, *ad nauseam*, were in the mail. A doctor's bill arrived the second month in response to treatment for a shoulder contusion I had sustained while heroically breaking the fall of a branch from our new, self-trimming tulip tree. With the self-trimming feature, at least we saved on the tree surgeon. . . . Ah, well! So much for the joys of home ownership, and also for the new addition that had been tentatively scheduled to be framed and under roof by our second month of occupancy.

After ten years in that house I was well on the way to master contractor status as a painter, plumber, mechanic, carpenter, etc.— a jack-of-all-trades—you name it! I was in the home improvement business and didn't know it. I'd cornered the market; or, rather, the market had cornered me, since my portfolio consisted of only a single property—my house. It was inspiring to think, however, that it all had started with the simple hanging of a few pictures that first week. From the size nail holes I was making hanging pictures, by the second week I was an accomplished plasterer, good to repair any wall in town. Spotty finances forced me into a Time-Life Home Improvement book subscription. From there, simple wiring became simpler. I hammered some nails and built a birdhouse or two—for practice, mind you. After the formative years of puttering with odds and ends, I got the feel of things and, naturally, just kept rehabbing stuff into the next four decades. I was ready to slow down. At sixty-five everything I did felt like slow motion or a bad dream. That, coupled with my wife's innate negativism, made my decision easy. I would retire on two fronts.

Think again, pal!

By chance, some new neighbors got wind of my in-house labors and asked to see my work. Soon—at least once a week—my wife was showing our place like it was Frank Lloyd Wright's *Fallingwater*. The neighborhood was in awe of my home improvement skills. Friends of neighbors began calling for estimates to build a deck, or install windows, or to just recommend and assist in projects already underway. Without moving a finger, I had an instant backlog. The sheer luck of being "discovered" was astounding. My view of retirement took on a whole new light. With luck, I could be spending my twilight years on profit and pleasure. Most mornings after that my wife spent her early hours hanging over the back fence, either "in session" with the neighborhood wives, or donating my "professional" expertise to the first bidder. Coming from her mouth, nothing was beyond my skills—no job too complex. The neighbors had only to name their project for instant assurance that I was their man: patios, wallpaper, drywall, ceramic tile, skyscrapers, national monuments, etc. I was forced to step in when serious talk began about widening the Panama Canal (just kidding—but you get the point).

Credit really belongs, then, to my charming wife for my life's final development and success. Her crowning praise of my existence happened each morning. Meeting with the local ladies in the back yard, she unfailingly prefaced her daily remarks with a beaming smile and the brash admission to have practically been sleeping with Bob Vila in a king-sized bed ever since Eisenhower's second term in the White House.

These days couples march to a different drum. Cash money's a thing of the past. It's only for pocket change—not crucial for getting by, or for eking it out. Amazingly blase' amid serious things, from ignorance, perhaps, of obligation, they're practically in denial of life's next move, be it up or down: If the bottom falls out, call home. If home gives a busy signal shrug it off. Find a cheap lawyer—charge the fee to the folks—and file the proper papers in bankruptcy, making certain to retain all "luxury" assets so to live in the style of one's custom as one moves on. After that . . . do it again, and again . . . and again. Safety nets today come in all quantities and sizes.

It seems that young couples today practically start out at pubescence. Dutifully, they hire consultants to advise on the trendiest options against conjugal living (the barbaric ritual called marriage is hardly a fitting choice, having been summarily rejected as the affliction of religious fanatics and dolts). The goal in these enlightened times is a true "limited, or no liability" partnership—a "break away" arrangement of sorts. There must be a pre-nuptial arrangement (how else to divide the Lego's, Game Boy's and Play Station's?). A small thing often overlooked in these affairs is the imprint L.L.P. on family stationary, assuming they own stationary and are fluent with words and can actually read and write. Hyphenated names, while okay, are usually at the insistence of the female partner who must retain her surname, and thus her individuality, at any cost-- even if it does happen to be Lipshitz. Most important, in relations with strait-laced neighbors and friends, is the unflinching appearance of propriety, wealth and the "we-don't-give-a-crap-what-you-think" attitude, particularly when deciding to birth and raise accidentally conceived children. Nowadays, the sudden appearance of babies tends to tarnish many young parents' supremely cherished image of independence.

The usual scenario is to buy a pair of expensive cars, select an appropriate up-scale neighborhood, spend half a year picking out furniture, wallpaper and drapes, and then commandeer four or five moving vans to a twenty room Georgian colonial in some gated community—definitely near *his* golf club, and a stone's throw from *her* spa, tennis club and psychic advisor. They purchase a "coterie" of pets—all neutered. She generally bonds with an expensive, slinky, sneaky, aloof Persian cat, as well as some miniscule poodle or terrier. He, on the other hand, usually displays his mastery over the meanest looking rottweiler in captivity. They both work, appearing as "briefcase carrying" professionals to the neighborhood. The children, if any, attend Day Care. Girl children take dance lessons; boy children learn karate (or another form of martial arts designed for possible future defense against a raging rottweiler). Professional landscapers do the lawn and garden. A local "pool maintenance" firm opens, closes and cleans the backyard swimming pool each spring and fall. Do-it-yourself projects are limited to using the family John Deere-V8 tractor for cutting grass, and an 85 HP, commercial snow blower to clear the driveway each winter.

I don't begrudge young couples their good fortune today. I simply wonder how the hell they pull it off.

Chapter Six

Like, Love, Marriage and Then Some

"I think you're gorgeous, you're charming, you're stunning,
you're perfect,
And then some.
You got me dazzled, and frantic, excited, romantic,
And then some...
I'll be your shadow, your slavey, your Army and your Navy,
And then some.
'Cause you're gorgeous, you're charming, you're stunning,
you're perfect,
And then some."[4]

Forgive this senior moment, but: "Is it not strange that desire should so many years outlive performance?"[5]

The first perception of retirement is about sex. Instantly it's there: the notion of "experienced," married adults—no kids or pets to avoid—romping for days and nights and weeks, from room to room, in wild, rampant, uninhibited sex. Forget that both participants are sixty five and overweight and bent out of shape. Sex is ageless and adaptable to any size or form. We could die—in each other's arms . . . how classic—from exhaustion, malnutrition, or *decubitus* ulcers (just plain old bed sores doesn't cut it here). Not to fret, though. We have the market cornered on multi-vitamins and mineral water . . . with little survival packets of crackers and diet drinks stashed throughout the rooms. The fridge and cupboards are loaded "to the gunwales"; the microwave is food-laden and at "the ready" to be tripped by motion sensors the instant our "trysting tour" of the love nest reaches the kitchen and, amid festive banners and balloons, is ultimately consummated on a rock maple breakfast room table where, afterwards, we'll devour tons of fresh bagels and marmalade to the strains of the final *Allegro* from Beethoven's String Quartet in A Major . . . spent. Overwhelmed by ecstasy, my wife's first breathless utterance will be: "The mattresses need flipped," and, "*oi* . . . with my back, thank God for ranch style and no stairs." I, on the other hand, will be thinking ponderously of outdoor pool facilities and surrounding structures—perhaps a tree house, or such—for subsequent adventures—weather permitting— into uncharted delights. Then, hallelujah, thinking further ahead: By alternating sex and cold showers far into our nineties, we could surpass the Fantastiks in performance longevity. At the end of our *golden years* one final burden will remain. We'll need a new game plan with the *platinum years* just ahead. By that time, however, wanting to avoid any serious relapse from old habits well learned, we'll be combat-ready—well read and probably board certified in viagraphy, the science of sexual stamina.

So goes the first perception of retirement. As for the next—it's still about sex: Better think this thing through. Were there orgies at twenty five?—or on the honeymoon? Was the word "orgy" even ever part of our common language? What exactly then, after forty-plus years of lukewarm intimacy, should suddenly transform this elderly housewife with arthritic knees into a Greek love goddess and pulsating Venus de Milo just because I decided to retire?

Ultimately, stage three—*actual* retirement—was upon us. Exactly ten minutes after our first *his and her* pension checks cleared the Federal Reserve Banking System, my former loving wife became "trouble and strife" and instantly took unilateral, multiple vows of chastity, sobriety and extreme morality (electronic banking and friendly contacts at the Fed made this all possible). I'd often suspected *some* spousal displeasure on her part, but never was sure. Sometimes overhearing her audible wish to rid the world of dirty old men, I often suspected she had a particular "dirtbag" in mind. So, now, without expecting it, I was about to go through the *real change of life*. Talk about being left in the lurch. Up to then I didn't know a lurch from rolled oats. Suddenly, I was in one (a lurch, not a rolled oat). Next, she took on the insufferable qualities of her long gone mother—a "classy" woman (a class of her own), gladly willing to endure "liars, and fools, and hypocrites"[6] and then kick a dog out of the house. Eventually, my wife was dressing like Mother Teresa. Formal visitation rights to consummate simple hand shakes—gloves optional—was practically the standing order of the day. As our relationship deflated I began seeing a mental image of her as the *possum*. At the slightest touch from any part of my body to any part of hers—in the dead of night or blinding light of day—she would assume a catatonic state that made Calvin Coolidge resemble a Lindy dancer with *delirium tremens*. Given the chance, for sure she could've outlasted the Great Sphinx of Egypt . . . had he been in the neighborhood, that is, expecting sexual favors. Eventually the *possum persona* gave way as she segued smoothly into *rigor mortis* for the living. If on some nights I attempted to outlast her *stupor*, instantly she was both out of the bed and the bedroom, flying off to attend to critically urgent chores. Forget that it could be two a.m. on a snowy winter morn. As she would aptly state: "When the oven needs cleaned or the toilets scoured, indeed, 'procrastination *is* the thief of time.'"[7]

In ordinary conversation, the two of us began sounding similar to fifty year-old reruns of the constant bickering bouts of my grandparents. There was one outstanding difference, however. Our versions lacked the blaring intensity of Grandma's and Grandpa's rounds, since Grandma was deaf—with or without a hearing aid—and Grandpa suffered from extreme obstinacy. By comparison, my wife is only partially deaf. I, on the other hand, embody the essence of statesmanship in all things. Reality for us, however, was setting in like super glue. Remembered attitudes and other day dreams were lost in our daily lives. Words and actions once taken for granted fell through the cracks. Frequently the moment dealt with a lost attitude toward whimsy . . . a sense of humor about sex. In the mornings, early in our marriage, she would often make our bed in the nude. I'd say: ". . . love the new maid's costume." With nary a pause she'd snap: "It's the new deep pocket model . . . just for you, sweetie." Or: "While I'm making the bed I can do the same for you, lover boy." Forty-five years later the same lady says: "Yea . . . maid. . . . You got that right! For once!" If there's a holy order somewhere out there known as The Sister's of the Keeper of the Cervical Seal, you can bet that the Keeper of the Key to that Seal has surely entrusted it to the bonded security of a certain founding member and Executrix of the Order, namely, my wife. In these later years my *haus frau* holds the original patent on retrofitted virginity. Where such feminine virtue abounds, one instantly imagines a defiled "tooth fairy" achieving parity with the "whore of Baghdad." My bride's a puzzle. It's what I call "and then some." The natural progression of male/female relations historically shows: We like, we love, we marry and then some. I'll deal with it.

A sexual revolution of sorts for most senior citizens alive and active today started sometime in the 1940s, the decade known as The Jive Generation. Because of World War II, as I remember, the process started rather respectfully, with patriotism and a sense of duty to country and all that we stood for. It ended with a bang (no pun intended) sometime during The Cool Generation. The so-called Cool Generation was the 1950s. That's when we completed *like* and graduated to *love*, finally settling for blissful *marriage*. During the '40s the word "sex" wasn't commonly spoken among twelve year olds. Generally, it was a word slightly taboo even in "polite," more mature circles. To borrow a '90s term: In the '40s, and maybe even into the '50s, the entire sexuality thing had an aura of "political correctness" (PC) about it. Yet it's strange. Today everything gets PC spin . . . *except* sex. During most of the Jive Generation we were a small town, Pennsylvania family living in the "wilds" of Baltimore, Maryland. My brother Frank and I spent most free time as "accepted" members of Cahill Center, a neighborhood youth activities organization. Young Baltmoreans (Baltimorons) weren't shy about branding a social peer as unpopular. To them unpopularity was a "tough role." They called every such person anything from a "creep" to a "zombie" to "gruesome" to a "square from Delaware." "Tough role" (or roll?) in those days was the teenage answer to any argumentative or combative situation that surfaced. Any guy not considered "smooth," "hep" or "groovy" by his young equals usually had a random, back alley chance to redeem his social status through a test of physical skills against a "rep" from the neighborhood "welcoming committee." Coming as we did from a family where weekly Sunday School and church was *the* option of choice and the strongest, in-home word ever uttered was "shucks," at first glance Frank and I probably were in for a "tough role." We didn't know it and never dwelled on it. There was never a problem, though. Our "press clippings" no doubt preceded us. (As explanation, this was not a "gang" as we know today. No laws were ever broken—except from random mischief. We all lived in the neighborhood. The girls weren't "molls." The age group at Cahill was from ten to eighteen years, although in the early '40s most seventeen and eighteen year olds were in military service. Any "hanky-panky" around was *strictly a private deal*. Compared to similar youth activity fifty and sixty years into the future, ours was a romp through Eden amid the apple blossoms.) The "committee" had an acceptance program based on physical and athletic ability, plus affinity for the female gender. The girls usually came around later for "personality testing" during the Cahill games and dances. Younger brother David's indoctrination was different. At age seven or eight years, Davey was being inadvertently "trained" from the ground up by the guys on the block. When not at Cahill the guys usually hung around various neighborhood porches and sidewalks conducting descriptive "bull sessions" about everything in particular and nothing in general. Davey would wander innocuously into the sinful midst of these "language seminars." After a few "classes," as we learned, he was mouthing perfectly, every dirty word in the book. The "f - word" seemed particularly attractive. Never did he give a finer soliloquy than on one summer evening during supper. Mother, I'm sure, was thankful that Dad was working late. After a detailed response to Mother's question: "How was your afternoon, David?"—in which he described as "f 'ing", everything from his scraped knee to the neighbor's dog—he asked for a second helping of "more 'f 'ing' waffles," as well as another glass of "godd—n, 'f 'ing' lemonade, please." As I choked and gagged and practically fell under the kitchen table from embarrassment, my mother never flinched. Reacting as if hearing a recitation from *A Child's Garden of Verses,* she served up another waffle and more lemonade, then calmly spoke: " David, those are not nice words. Please don't say those words again." Perfecto! . . . And the end of little brother David's short journey into foul mouthery.

My circle of friends was into the jive/swing/jitterbug culture. At the time we were too young or immature, or the wrong color, for the "bebop" culture. Words and actions then were so different from today. In 1946 changes in lifestyles abounded as the war was almost over and our servicemen began coming home. The term *teenager* had been around since the 1920s but it came into its own during the '40s. The young teenager was a separate and independent culture, generally not rebellious or subversive. In our actions we used expressive—almost always clean in mixed company—language, and stayed relatively polite and civilized. Attractive females of our age group could be called: drape shape, dilly, or "so round, so firm, so fully packed . . ." (borrowed from a Lucky Strike cigarette ad of the period); or for unattractive: battle, scrag or crate. Girls referred to attractive boys as: B.T.O. (big time operator), P.C. (prince charming), swoony, Jackson, drooly; or as unattractive: dogface, void coupon, sad Sam, stud (oaf). Hello's and good-bye's consisted of: "Hi, sugar. Are you rationed?", "What's knitten', kitten?", "Plant you now, dig you later.", "Bye-bye, buy bonds." or "Aw reservoir."[8]

"Relationship" is a common buzz word these days. It implies marriage-like, very personal "goings-on" between couples—usually male and female. If you talked of "relationships" fifty years ago you were apt to be a genealogist discussing a certain family tree. Also, in those times, when young couples "clicked," people called it "love at first sight." With the modern "in crowd" that's a phrase to create barrels of laughs. Now it's likely "your place or mine" followed by "sex at first sight" and "love as a last resort." In the '40s and '50s (and prior) a regular occurrence was a marriage between "high school sweethearts," many of which remain intact to this day. The "one mate for life" tenet was often an inborn instruction from parents to children in those days. Marriages weren't exactly "arranged," but "suggested" marriage guidelines often were handed down by caring elders. It's fair to say that certain parents would never hold back a "full court press" when a "hot prospect" was invited to the house for dinner by a son or daughter. "One mate for life" is *apropos* of nature. With modern couples it's the only animal instinct not observed.

As we moved into the 1950s, the "like" period was over for most and the action was warming into the "love" period. Brother Frank always had a nice "package" on his arm at the local YMCA dances. Many were dating steady or, at least, had one or two serious liaisons. The drive-in movie was a favorite pastime for daring double-daters (more on that later). High school was getting over for most. Many looked forward to college. Korea was in the picture as well. As a rule—possibly to our chagrin—despite the turmoil around us, we stayed with our roots and true to ourselves.

By the mid-to-late '50s most of us were through with "love" and onto marriage, children and a career. The time-line of our sexual revolution was about to reach high gear, sweeping us into the 1960s on the crest of a "cultural" tidal wave that was affecting the world as we knew it—in morals, manners, language— you name it. At a movie theater a kissing scene, once tender and subdued, e.g., perhaps between Charles Boyer and Ingrid Bergman in *Gaslight*, was now re-enacted by two freaks on the screen swabbing tonsils and speaking lines like: ". . . alive in the '60s is *too* fabulous to endure. . . . French kissing is so cleansing, so . . . *mature*!"

Maturity, we found, had nothing to do with it. Enter . . . Hugh Hefner and the Playboy Empire. Here comes this introverted kid from Chicago, probably without a date in his life; suddenly he's America's celebrated expert on "hot babes." From day one his *Playboy* Magazine aimed for cultural inroads; in truth, it was always a "girlie" gazette pure and simple. It still is, except that nowadays stores keep it out of sight in a plain brown wrapper lest the modern "artistic pap" displayed therein should tend to pervert the kiddies and "snuff" the geezers. *Playboy's* subtle approach was always laudable: After a centerfold of dazzling, full frontal nudity—plus a *col-*

lage ad lib of stirring selections depicting, for instance, a former Mennonite lass turned Corporate CEO posing in the buff amid splayed palm fronds and obsolete office equipment—a few "serious" articles surfaced randomly. These essays, normally authored by some "expert" of general sorts, served as a kind of literary "cold shower" between remaining clinical "babe sessions" yet to be eyeballed. Other than the pleasure of ogling the many great nude shots of the magazine, *Playboy* was never an avid experience for me. "Serious" content in the magazine, for me, usually recalled some inane analysis of odd or worthless knowledge, something akin to: "The Lost Art of the Slide Rule," authored by some sad emeritus professor of engineering somewhere, or "Truth in Advertising: Why Lucky Strike Green Never Went to War," etc., and so on. Lots of copycat publications followed *Playboy*. I remember a girlie magazine piece (*Playboy* or otherwise), way back, on the actress, Grace Kelly. Some brilliant screenwriter surveying past movie queens described her as having a "smoldering sexuality." What the hell is *smoldering sexuality* anyhow? Where do they contrive such phony, Loreleian[9] tripe. Grace Kelly was great—believable and classy, unlike most Hollywood "queens" of this era; but between the pages of a "skin journal" wasn't her best side.

I never cared for *Playboy* after the "bunnies" came full circle to total nudity. The tease appeal was lost. Gone was the feminine mystique; here to stay was the female body *a la* Gray's Anatomy. When you've seen one pubic region, you've seen'em all. Overnight, the magazine became a pale version of *National Geographic.* Ubiquitous tours of the mansion and bevy-filled pool became stale, as good old Hef and his perpetual robe, slippers, pipe and *tart du jour* always gazed out on the filial frolics with sage approval. Hefner always looked so studious in pajamas, hanging around the mansion all day with his top heavy ladies—sort of like Mr. Chips indoctrinating the first co-ed class at "jolly, ole' Brookfield." One almost could read his thoughts: "Those 'schmucks' from the old neighborhood should see me now!"

Movie production contributed big time to the sexual revolution in the '60s. Most films concentrated on a standard formula of "no plot and gratuitous sex." The updated bedroom scene was typical: In the old versions all the action stayed behind closed doors to a background of soft music and fading lights. This approach gave an appearance of impropriety to the new Hollywood savants. Since the audience already knew the couple were both double agents about to exchange nuclear secrets, let the doors stay open. Keep it obvious. Move the plot along. Let them have an orgy for the world to see—keep things natural and above board. It's acceptable and expected behavior.

The Internet has been the absolute toppler of sexual mores at the dawn of our new century. The number of web sites dedicated to pornography these days is inestimable. Try going on line and entering the key word "sex" or any variation thereof. Unless you're on the so-called "cutting edge" of computer technology, it's likely that a full download of the results would declass your machine into a great time warp of obsolescence. Forget that their are countless web sites; think instead of the thousands of links to each site. Ring that up on your abacus and you'll see that Generation-X is in big, big trouble. As an example: A few years ago while looking for the site of Ashlea Furniture, incorrectly, I keyed in "Ashley." In a gnat's instant I was welcomed to the site of some super babe called Ashley S____, whose credentials (with pictures and description) included participation in the great Nevada Sex-a-Thon, i.e., live sex entertainment, which is legal in Nevada. The purpose of subject sex-a-thon was to break the world's record for the female having the most sex partners at one sitting (so to speak). Participants included porno stars, brothel employees and rank amateurs. The public reaction to this stuff was and is: "Ho hum . . . just another day at the bordello. A day without sex is like a day without sex."

The real problem is control and supervision. Even without the Internet we have big problems protecting our children from unreined debauchery, with such "well-intentioned idiots" as the Federal Public Health Service out there setting teenage guidelines like distributing condoms and using bananas to teach proper condom application and wear. Abstinence—when considered—is supported by recommending masturbation and oral sex as safe sex, or non-sex— even suggesting flavored condoms to prevent *halitosis* (bad breath sounds so gauche to medical people). And incidentally—based on recent agriculture economic indicators—bananas are in demand again.

The nightmare of modern sexual practice is in its extremes, as is the perturbing fact of easy access to this stuff, along with the lah-di-dah attitude of the public at large to dismiss it as so much "boys and girls-will-be-boys and girls" *falderal*. At the opposite pole are certain people—usually females—who take on monumentally prudish airs to fend off male oriented comments suggesting that they may be a credit to their gender. Recently, after an attempt by some entity at CNN to spice up a Paula Zahn TV promo by calling her "sexy," the earth almost moved. It became a media "event" for a day or two. Unfortunately, Ms. Zahn started off by being livid and affronted. At once her superiors acted embarrassed and apologetic, vowing "we'll get to the bottom of this travesty," or words to that effect. It's a sad fact that we live in an era where things like public "quadruple 'X' live porno" shows involving females are as common as dandruff, with certain women and men being more than willing participants. For the price of admission other women and men gladly attend these events. Except for sequestered nuns high in the Andes, most woman in the world also know that the twenty-first century hosts a veritable sewer of prurient activity. Who among us speaks out in protest? Certainly no female—or feminist—group that I know of. My point is: When will self-styled females deign to accept a compliment and stop acting the panicked Victorian virgin in an unlocked chastity belt. Ms. Zahn, for one, *is* sexy and should stand and take a bow for it. The same goes for thousands more of the "sexy" female persuasion, regardless of age, color, creed, religion or ethnic background. The whole modern feminist movement is a sham, forgetting that ". . . on the highest throne in the world we are still sitting on our own ass."[10] Dismay is expressed only when a situation is politically expedient. The avowed feminists missed their grand stand at outrage when "Clinton and cronies" happened by for eight years. In an unvarnished historical context, the frequency of "Slick Willie's" alleged offenses against the female anatomy suggests that, by comparison, Attilla the Hun possibly should be downgraded to "unconfirmed village eunuch." Given more years for more lust in office, Clinton could've easily approved legislation and made it as the first "protectee" in a federally funded Lechers Protection Program. Now there's a legacy for ya'.

Driving the cycle of sex is *like, love, marriage* and *then some*. As with the free lunch, *innocence* is gone forever.

Chapter Seven

Self Improvement

"Once I built a railroad,
Made it run,
Made it race against time.
Once I built a railroad,
Now it's done,
Brother, can you spare a dime?"[11]

Vicariously—for the past fifty years—I've lived the role of a slob, reasoning that the rare life experiences of hoboes, derelicts and little kids have always been so unfairly withheld from much of our population. Voluntary dishevelment to this day remains one of my self-considered, secret, exalted "states of grace." During a lifetime of school and business commitments, in the face of standing orders to be always on call—mostly in suit, tie and white dress shirt—I was forever enthralled with the slovenly way. From the age of about fifteen, with some necessary exceptions, I was never privileged to wear just plain "overalls" (never called dungarees or jeans) as just general attire. During grade school I did wear "knickers." A pair of knickers was a good second choice. Though semi-dressy, given enough wear, they could get just as sloppy and comfortable as a raggy pair of overalls. No self-respecting, red-blooded American boy, however, would be caught dead in knickers beyond the eighth grade. As a youth in my parents house, appearance and cleanliness was next to godliness, along with "proper things," meaning good manners and proper grammar and respectable language. Totally unfair by modern day standards, I know.

Sartorial reformation never happened for me until after the aforementioned "fifty years" and my official retirement from the working world and the formality therein. By then, however, powers in the business world had decided that in the work place a much looser, relaxed dress code was just the right ticket to foster a consistently good employee morale. That's when the offices and executive suites got into "dress down" days and other fashion atrocities. Meanwhile, on the street, teenagers and young adults also shifted priorities as they created a continuing image of style and deportment *a 'la* Afghan cave dwellers. Swishy designers even get awards these days for the burlap and denim they pass off as a "fashion statement." Thus, society has come full circle. Today the "slobovian" lifestyle is legit. My chance to be different, to compete and fulfill the slovenly dream has come and gone, since even I haven't the guts to appear publicly in the fashion extremes of this day. Around the house now I wear simple things: an old sport shirt, overalls and a baseball hat. On special days I'm in clean overalls—now called dungarees or jeans—and a different baseball hat. I shave when necessary and every two months get a haircut. Personal hygiene is attended to daily. Typically, for a lifetime, such dilemmas of "time and place" have dogged me: When the pro scouts needed pitchers, I was a catcher; during Korea when I joined the Navy for aerial photography, they had a shortage of medics and my pre-med background was their beacon in the night; after years of honing a fine palate for *Oysters Bienville*, the Chesapeake Bay went suddenly sour and regressed to a giant quagmire of fatal oyster *fungi*. My second goal of retirement was not to be. I would never be the professional slob of my fabled dreams.

Granted, there were minor compensations on the way to retirement—most coming since my wedding day—from a woman who could make me feel like a real slob. From the day my wife and I vowed "I do," it was chaos. Oh, the mini inquisitions I endured . . . the needling questions. She had a penchant for "do ya' know" stuff. Things like: "Do ya' know a dirty clothes hamper when ya' see it?" or, "Do ya' know about the new Vo-Tech course on reloading empty toilet paper holders?" or, "Do ya' know we own a toilet now that actually flushes?" In retirement I've vowed to reward my exasperated bride with a "brand new me" in a brand new package. Sometime years ago I muttered "for better or for worse." Presumably from past criticism, she's had enough "for worse." So now as I roll out the "for better" she will instantly appreciate that I've captured the combined essence of Prince Valiant, Mr. Rogers and his neighborhood, and Bishop Fulton J. Sheen into my new *persona*. It'll be worth more than gold for her . . . for our . . . fiftieth anniversary year. Naturally, if the "new me" doesn't fit the bill I'll get a bulldog as my "babe magnet" and hang out at Pet Smart with the other geezers—the old guys with pants hitched up to the armpits—looking for furry lap dogs towing blue-haired "dowager types" on a leash.

I'm improving in other ways, too, ways that, at first, strike some humans as strange. In younger days I ogled pretty girls and browsed newsstands for girlie magazines. Now I ogle recipes and buy cook books and look regularly for my "choice dishes" on The Food Channel, i.e., *Coq au Vin, Boeuf Bourguignon*, etc. Nowadays, I love to "cook out" on the patio. It's not just a reason to drink beer and watch the steaks burn, anymore. Cooking out is actually fun. Speaking of beer: In my German dotage I've come to regard beer as food (as all good *Deutschlanders* eventually should and must). Gone are the reckless, beer guzzling sprees of my past. Actually, it never was "cool" to simply drink to get drunk. I never have. There were occasions, I'll admit, when being "overserved" became somewhat troublesome (to cite the late comedian, George Gobel). Since retirement, my wife and I eat at a good restaurant at least once a week. We both are ex-smokers. I smoked heavily and still harbor a soft spot for those addicted to the "cancer weed." Most restaurants still cater to both smokers and non-smokers, though they practice a sinister form of discrimination: Non-smokers are summarily assigned seating in the darkest, remotest sections of the restaurant, areas where the waiters stroll through about every other hour to announce: "It'll just be a few minutes more." Restaurant SOP these days is to seat smokers and their smoke at the best tables in the house, far away from the *sterility and rarified air* of the kitchen area, a spot where half the cooks often look like "typhoid Mary's" council-in-waiting. It gets ridiculous enough at some eateries to practically drive one back to cigarettes, until you recall how it really was to be addicted. The fact of cigarette addiction is probably child's play compared to the gruesome hell for a drug addict to sustain a daily habit. Putting out money every day—having to get the money everyday—has to be horrible. Every kid in America needs to hear the true facts about drugs from the earliest age of understanding. I can only relate to a three pack-a-day cigarette habit which I quit cold turkey twenty-five years ago after verging on a serious illness.

During my working years I never could fulfill certain self-interests. So rightfully, in body and spirit, I've become obsessed with accomplishment and respectability. Through forty years as a financial manager I had acquired knowledge of things that are now, at age sixty-five, at best of marginal use. The one exception is my mechanical skill which always has and will be my ace-in-the-hole. Now for the first time in my life I'm free to do it my way. My wife at first was concerned that I set a good example and avoid a reputation as the village idiot. On that note I made her my "official" Director of Public Relations with orders to keep a finger on the pulse of "village" opinion. I pondered the question of writing and "how does a person become a writer?" Someone said that if one arises each morning and writes, he or she is considered a writer. So whada'ya' know: one problem solved.

At my age, the perceived betterment of mind over body involves combating the younger, more liberal types who call me "pops" and "geezer" and take me for the end-product of an out-patient, frontal lobotomy clinic. Meanwhile, they and friends and causes go merrily along, running roughshod over, through and around a punchboard of traditional values most traditional Americans have championed for decades. I've taken my case to the op-ed page, attacking "ridiculous" issues which I fear could become sublime, or where "sublime" should be fingered as ridiculous. The process is a tonic. Knowing that the public airing of your five hundred, precisely chosen words can instantly influence opinions at a thousand breakfast tables, or in local shops and salons, or on busy street corners, is like giving birth. At times it's like passing a kidney stone. I get cheers and jeers from my public. Either way there's a give and take of ideas . . . of public opinion, a real grass-roots show of freedom of speech. Where else but in America? . . . It all has a positive effect. Regardless of accusations that I'm an idiot, or the fatherless offspring of prairie dogs, I'm delighted for the ability to stir emotions as I write and learn. The topics are endless:

<u>Road Rage 101</u>— Senior drivers everywhere are coming under the scrutiny of state transportation departments. This is a good thing, aimed at protecting all drivers from us geezers who may have become mentally and/or physically inept, and, therefore, a risk behind the steering wheel of today's supercharged speed machines. On the other hand, safety is one goal; "rules-of-the-road and driver etiquette" is another.

Despite the presence of mature age and old fogyism, most of the time I can read and spell and reason beyond the fourth grade level. Younger drivers on the road—and others—these days very often can not. "Yield"—if they know it to be a word from the English language—usually translates to: "We gonna' play chicken with this sucker." The typical driver in the uninterrupted traffic lane in construction areas interprets "Merge left or right" as: "Close it up, *stat*—bumper to bumper. I got the right of way, and I ain't gonna' give it up." "Slow" covers any speed between 50 and 60 mph. The posted speed limit, anywhere, means: Always add at least 10 mph to the legal limit. Turn signals are for Amish buggies. And a yellow traffic signal is automatic for "go like hell, the red light's coming." The best—or worst, depending on point of view—is the souped-up "classic" just managing a screeching halt behind you at a busy intersection. At the controls of said "junk pile"—with boom box resonating enough bass to unglue your dental work—the driver, this ace among men (or women), is ever vigilant to give you the horn, lights and upthrust fist—with finger patriotically offering half-a-peace sign—for even the slightest delay in his, or her, busy schedule. To avoid such rage and hostility you must instantly shift into afterburner mode and be thrusting at about two G's during the first four nano seconds after the light turns green. You must understand, after all, that certain drivers today are desperately pressed for time—poor dears—and insist that you should know it. Once you've removed your "impediment" from their immediate driving line, jauntily they roar, squeal and screech off into traffic . . . likely just to be *cool* . . . continuing to ignore every rule and courtesy in the book. Most folks of all ages are upstanding individuals when they're at home or at church or at play. Judged by their driving sense, however, some would do better in a vat of formaldehyde with other undeveloped species.

State government should wake up and make Driver Education a four year mandatory, comprehensive course in our high schools. Compared to four years of Gym class, future returns in lives saved and egos salved will be far greater.

A "Liberal" Liberal Arts Education — I sense the beginning of a trend in college English literature curricula these days in that recent thinking would cherish the propriety of modern writers while ignoring the time tested classicists. Toni Morrison *et al* would be mandatory; Shakespeare *et al* would be consigned to some optional grab bag. It's a mindset that would replace nuclear physics with "connect-the-dots." As with all great literary minds, the classicists were more than entertaining writers. They were thinkers and thought provokers. Most could analyze the subtleties of an emotion and produce enough material for a two volume set or a three act play. And, unlike many modern writers, they could even do it without smothering us in the "reality" of several hundred gratuitous obscenities per sentence. Ms. Morrison is typical of today's fine writers, not to be disparaged. By comparison, however: What lately have they done Shakespearean?

Over time, this growing trend will add new meaning to "a strong *liberal* arts education."

Whose God Is It, Anyway? — Recently, a small, Pennsylvania church raised a local furor as the result of a well publicized "media burning" of their own property, on their own property. Those involved stressed that the "burning" wasn't an attempt to impose their beliefs and values on the public-at-large. They burned only their own property at the urging of *their* God.

Whose God is it, anyway—theirs, ours, yours or mine? Regardless, today we fill life's blanks with good intentions and call our actions the will of God. Those church folks didn't burn books to impose their values on an unsuspecting public. But their intolerance was out there for the world to see. It's the random spark that starts the fire.

<u>Gimmee A Break</u> — Whatever happened to the America we once knew? How is it that anybody and his brother can object to the public display of something, even remotely religious, as being offensive and have it removed from sight, *tout a' l'heure*? But . . . if I complain about the Adult "Entertainment" Store that just opened on my street, I'm violating some whacko's First Amendment rights.

Forty years ago we'd be running these bums out of town on a rail.

<u>Stay The Course</u> — Some time ago, a Lancaster, Pennsylvania mayor jokingly offered to get certain local high school students a Monopoly token as their reward for perfect class attendance. When he off-handedly suggested a "get-out-of-jail-free" card, they were offended. It . . . "played to the errant perception that many teenagers at McCaskey H. S. are felons."[12] The mayor promptly apologized.

Now, because of the flak raised by a few students (or their parents?), a new perception of certain, supposedly mature, high schoolers comes to mind: They are certifiable, "thin-skinned cry babies" surely deserving of either a "get real" card, or a "get a life" card.

Any serious person faulting the spoken reference to a parlor game card, a line that's been bandied about in good fun for seventy years, would just as likely label Lincoln's Gettysburg Address: "inflammatory and a blight on dead heroes." Talk about your hypocrisy: It's Orwell's insidious "thought police" in action. The wrong party got the apology. And if I may say—without playing to errant perceptions—somewhere the inmates are running the asylum. Given the state of today's moral habits, had the mayor's throwaway jest been wrapped between three or four obscenities, one can easily imagine his would-be critics suddenly in awe of his down-to-earth qualities, giving him "high fives" and lauding him as "a true visionary" among men and the people.

The entire incident reeks of a politically motivated situation. If politicians want to slam politicians, we should insist they do it on the issues—not masked as some stupid, infantile, contrived affront by school boys. We used to portray our governing elders as role models, treating them with a semblance of manners, ethics and fair play. We used to have a sense of humor, too.

Stay the course, Mr. Mayor!

<u>Un-Americanism 101</u> — The following concerns an op-ed piece entitled "Would bin Laden be a Republican?" and my response to it: The recent letter . . . is as vile a hate piece as I've read anywhere. It is, however, typical of a political philosophy that has gripped America for the last decade, coming almost direct from the grotesque mindset of a James Carville or Paul Begala. Even *those* two goons, since 9-11, have had the sense to "button it." Be mindful that bin Laden is a maniacal mass murderer intent upon worldwide destruction of all religious beliefs but his own. To suggest a commonality between such vermin and certain American citizens—notwithstanding the President of the United States of any party affiliation—is almost akin to an accusation of aiding and abetting treason. Where is the writer's sense of decency? September 11 cured much of this type of un-Americanism. It appears that pockets of resistance still exist.

I regret being unable to afford at this time, a one-way fare for Mr. T———'s destination of choice—preferably outside American borders. Is it true, I wonder, that falling on one's pointy head during the cloning process is cause for acute stupidity in certain lab specimens?

At this point in my days I'm neither a quirk nor a curmudgeon. For the good of the cause, i.e., freedoms to exercise intellectual curiosity and to tell political correctness gurus: "Go flush," I'm into advocacy—working up to *Advocate First Class*—of the "conservative lifestyle and thought brigade." This on the fervent belief that since the mid 1960s the modern power structure of American liberalism, through a spate of questionable (at best) "grand ideas and causes," has been leading the greatest nation in the history of civilization down a deliberate, pernicious garden path to a doomsday future. Sadly, it's all about job security and dynasty building into the next millenium and beyond through liberal "power" politics. Recent advice by Chris Matthews—host of Hard Ball (CNBC)—to Democrats/liberals on turning a national business disaster (Enron) into a political scandal was yet another example of a media maven continuing to play the fool. Matthews, connoisseur of distorting the obvious, laid out his three-step "strategy": "Shoot to kill! . . . Place the blame humbly and smartly on the Republicans. . . . Tie it all together."[13] What stunning insensitivity! At first glance it appeared to be a joke. Media bias these days is simply chock full of unbrilliant, unobjective, unstatesmenship-like rules to live by. Consider a few more recent examples of "liberal logic," some of which (cited) have been excerpted from the Media Research Center's annual awards for the most outrageous news quotes of year 2001:

Education: Year after year as liberal legislators continue to appropriate an annual twenty billion dollars toward American education, the inflow of dues to teacher's union coffers gets an "A" for *astronomical*. Quality and standards in the class room continue to "flat line" and get "F" for *failing*.

Animal Rights: PETA (People for the Ethical Treatment of Animals) "It would be great if all the fast-food outlets, slaughterhouses, these laboratories and banks who fund them exploded tomorrow."[14]

Conservation: GREENPEACE ". . . a band of scientific illiterates who use Gestapo tactics . . ."[15]

Global Warming: ". . . and you wonder what's it gonna take. I mean, is it gonna take some kind of real catastrophe? I mean, does an iceberg have to come floating down the Hudson before somebody stands up and goes, 'Oh, yeah'?"[16] What happened to the "global cooling" theory these nuts were foisting a few decades back?

Taxation: Senator Tom Daschle (D.-S.D.) recently made the outlandish claim that the Bush Administration tax cut had actually made the 2001/2002 recession worse by eliminating the budget surplus and causing long-term interest rates to rise. Mr. Daschle needs a refresher course in Math and Economics.[17] Interest rates have actually fallen during the Bush presidency; and the tax cut was much too small to make even a dent in the surplus. Besides, as of the date of Daschle's criticism, seventy five percent of the tax cut wouldn't take effect until the next four to six years. With added audacity, he proclaimed that the recession was actually a "Bush recession," despite having started at the end of Clinton's term—sometime between August, 2000, and January, 2001. With such affinity for comic relief, Mr. Daschle may yet comment on South Dakota's improved quality of life in terms of key economic indicators which show South Dakota "outhouse" keepers now preferring the L. L. Bean catalog over Sears as the "necessary paper" of choice.

Just Pure Hatred: Bill Maher, host of ABC's "Politically Correct": "I do think, if it turns out that, this beautiful young girl is gone, I think, and he [Rep. Gary Condit] is responsible in some way, you have to look to Ken Starr for some guilt."

Larry King: "Why?"

Maher: "Because, you know, Ken Starr made it so that you, in the old days, you had an affair with somebody, and you know, okay, you had an affair. The press didn't report it. They didn't make a political criminal case of it. Now, it's almost like you have to get rid of them."[18]

One More, Mount Rushmore! or, Chiseling a Chiseler: "Throughout his eight years in office, President Clinton warned us that the next great menace was international terrorism. . . . He also brought unprecedented prosperity to our nation, and because of that, President [Bush] can use the surplus Mr. Clinton left behind to pay for many of the nation's needs in this time of crisis. . . . This lecture series is about the human spirit. To me and millions of others, President Clinton has always personified that. He is a man from Hope, and that is what he has given us, hope. We miss him. Thank you, Mr. President."[19]

Speak for yourself, Helen (Thomas). On more than a few instances of international terrorism, Mr. Clinton certainly did warn us. A strange variety of "cryptic" signals it was, too: a stray missile here, a trailer park trashed there . . . a stained dress? . . . Well . . . you can see where this is going.

Wouldn't *just the truth* be a grand improvement for a change?

Chapter Eight

Movies

Excuse the overstatement but the last time I enjoyed a movie . . . in a regular theater, that is . . . was the year they increased adult admissions to twenty-five cents and stopped selling War bonds in the lobby. At any rate, I do know it was around the same time that Hollywood started giving its *wunderkinder*—those genius producers and screenwriters—a free hand to work their alphabetic magic on a mostly unsuspecting public. As loyal proponents of first amendment rights, these people proudly gave Americans a new version of on-screen reality with the ubiquity of the p-word, the s-word and that all time grabber . . . the f-word, foisting the verbal offspring of their new found constitutional freedom on us with the elegance of falling rocks. What a fine bunch of *linguists* these folks would become. Or, to paraphrase the Tommy Dorsey standard from 1941 (with Sinatra and Pied Pipers on vocal, nat'ch), "Oh! Look At Me Now"[20]:

"They never knew their technique was missing.

They never knew their skill was in blue sounding smut,
Just one of those ruts.
But, oh! Look at them now."

Since sometime around the so-called "cultural revolution" of the 1960s, I've been regularly distressed by the garbage that passes for entertainment. I know that I'm not alone. And yet, with a practiced recitation of feigned indignation, most purveyors of this trash will justify their "art form" to any critic. It starts with some knowing proclamation: *"This kinda shit really pisses me off! Don't'chya know we're just dealin' with reality here? Besides, they're only fuckin' words! Whad'ya want . . . real life or fuckin' fairy tales?"* Such abortion of purpose is the work of the devil to your average churchgoer, or faint of heart. But I agree totally with this deftly stated preamble. They are right on the money! They only write words! Believe me, just a bunch of rotten words! A recent survey on the personal traits of this country's elected officials listed a category titled: Most Frequent Use of Obscene Language. My first thought was: To be a 'top o' the Mark" foulmouth these days calls for some really fine tuned verbal and mental skills. Socially— quite predictably—foulmouthery has evolved into an involuntary speech impediment of the purest water. It's now more common than dirt. And unless one is taken for a Pentecostal and only sounds obscene, a true thoroughbred in the field *should* be awarded, at least, *some* public certification for dubious achievement. Fifty years ago, today's verbal obscenity addiction would have propelled the price of soap (the "wash your mouth out with" kind) into orbit. The good news is: SMUT spelled backwards is TUMS, an antacid and significant source of calcium for osteoporatic seniors in heat—sort of the *pill*, if you will, for horny geriatrics with gas. Gimmee a break! Whatever happened to the other six million words in the English language? It's strange that Webster and the other guys who do dictionaries get the "bum's rush" just because some *enlightened* movie moguls decided to *spin* The Bill of Rights for their own pleasure and profit.

Hypocrisy isn't my style—old fogyism is. I'm not a right-wing, religious whacko, either. I've heard *all* the dirty words. At times in my life I've even used them (but not all in a single sentence, contrary to the way of some *wortschmidts* around today). I'm an ex-sailor. Say no more. It's common knowledge that a tour with Uncle Sam's Navy isn't exactly a sabbatical for study and research of the *Bluejackets' Manual*. Military service presents some rowdy days. Make no mistake, opportunities abound there to perform in a lowlife circus, with mates and scuttlebutt so coarse that ". . . human language . . . is but little better than the croak and cackle of fowls."[21] Heaven forbid that parents could eavesdrop on those times in our lives—their demands for retroactive birth control would be universal. But eventually life leads us down a path to Yogi Berra's well publicized "fork in the road." And a smart lad of any day is well advised to take it, if only to heed the savvy advice of Professor Harold Hill of *Music Man* fame, the classic stage musical and movie, as he cautions the town fathers of River City, Iowa, on the evils of "pocket pool" versus the gentility of a "three rail shot" in the noble game of billiards:

"But just, as I say, it takes judgment, brains and maturity to score in a balkline game,
 I say that any boob kin take'n shove a ball in a pocket,
 And I call that sloth!
 The first big step on the road to the depths of degrada . . .
 I say, first, it's a little ah, medicinal wine from a teaspoon;
 Then beer from a bottle."[22]

Consider the movie houses of today. They're like Roman catacombs—practically endless—with untold numbers of cinematic caverns inside. Hollywood wasn't satisfied giving us only a few rotten films each week. They had to infuse us with daily doses of their middling slop. So now they shove them off the truck by the carton and into the local movie grottos faster than the "catacombs" can grow new space. And unless there's one with foreign sub-titles, they all start off with the same dandy dialogue, replete with every four-letter obscenity known to man or beast . . . stuff these screenwriting scribblers probably think they invented. And when their *verbiage garbage* eventually slimes in to overpower our collective psyche, the American theater-going public is deemed primed for Hollywood's next version of artistic muck. So bring on *erotica USA*! Oh, no! . . . Say it ain't so, Virginia! They're doing it right up there on the old silver screen . . . the exact spot where, as kids, we watched Roy and Gene and Hopalong make the Old West safe for school marms' and youngins'. . . where Gabby Hayes always complained to Roy, ". . . stop circlin' these dag'nabbed wagons, Roy, or we ain't never gonna' get to Californ'y." Once upon a time in movie production even the animals were chastised if they happened to ruin a scene with an *ad libbed*, on-camera, "call of nature." Now there's nothing *but* crap beyond the footlights.

Movies today aren't even close to the sheer excitement of the old World War II flicks: *Guadalcanal Diary* with William Bendix and Lloyd Nolan and all those nasty little Jap soldiers running through the jungle hiding out in coconut trees; or Don Ameche in *A Wing and A Prayer*; *Wake Island* starring Robert Preston; *The Purple Heart* with Richard Conte; Tom Neal in *First Yank Into Tokyo*; etc., etc., the list goes on and on. I remember *Air Force* with John Garfield and Harry Carey flying B-17's . . . and George Tobias' caustic words in the same movie after he polished off an enemy Zero over the Pacific: "Fried Jap going down." In 1946, when it cost the movie-going public about twenty-cents to watch a feature film, the news of the day, a cartoon and coming attractions, Hollywood was treating us to the best movies ever made in America. Consider that *The Best Years of Our Lives* won the Oscar that year. A couple runners-up were *To Each His Own* and *The Razor's Edge*—still gems to covet for a special TV evening at home. The next year brought classics like: *Gentleman's Agreement, The Farmer's Daughter, and Miracle On 34th Street*. And then into the '50s there was *The Quiet Man, Stalag 17* and *The African Queen*. Take your pick—treasures all—fit for the whole family and not a bum among'em. Choose any year up through 1960. The Hollywood hit parade never ended. For about the same price we pay now to mail a postcard, the movie makers were practically bombarding us with "Macy's bargain basement in spades" every day, in every village and town in America. Since the mid-1960s outstanding films have been rare. Most good ones have been musicals, or screen versions of Broadway hits, or both. Then again, nowadays, you need a supplemental home equity loan to afford tickets to any show, and—unless you brown bag it—a modest bank line of credit usually proves sufficient to purchase refreshments in the lobby. From there it goes down hill. Depending upon your "grotto" of choice and your threshold of pain, you can select from, maybe, thirty or so flicks—priced anywhere from five to ten dollars—with titles like *Vampires Suck* or *My Parents Were Lab Rats*, or *The Plastic Surgeon Who Hung Himself*. They wrote better stuff on the restroom walls in the El Patio Theater (Old Potato) when I was a kid in Tylertown, PA.

Thank God they tore down the "Old Potato" years ago—before this modern day debris littered the territory. It's sacrilege to imagine the vile reflection of even one of today's "R" or "X" rated *turkeys* up there occupying the same screen space where we watched our hallowed Hollywood heroes. Every Saturday afternoon in "living black and white," they gave us yet another offering—not just a paltry single, but a double dose—of their latest "masterpiece *du jour*," be it about war, the Old West or the Dead End Kids. It's hard to forget the raw excitement, the sounds and the smells, of that old threadbare movie palace. The screen lit up and came alive with Tarzan, Jane and Boy, and Flash Gordon capturing bad guys, or the screwball antics of Bud Abbot and Lou Costello, as well as the great tap routines of Bill "Bojangles" Robinson and little Shirley Temple.

They don't just talk garbage in films these days. They act it out, too, right up there in front of everybody . . . in front of your grandmother, your mother-in-law, your sister-in-law, your old Aunt Nellie . . . just everybody . . . while you're chewing on popcorn or sipping a soda. Once again, they call it reality. But it's all reversed today. Reality used to be taking your girl to a drive-in movie in your old man's car. That's when the popcorn and soda thing was, maybe, part of the screenplay and the "making out" part was, maybe, going on hot and heavy inside the parked cars *watching* the show. In those days, when you borrowed the family car, your parents always wanted to know stupid stuff like: *Where are you going tonight? Who with? When will you be back? Is your homework done?* If your night out involved a date at the drive-in, most parents practically wanted your signature on a performance bond stating that: (1) You were actually going to a drive-in; (2) The actual drive-in to which you actually were going, actually existed; and (3) You would actually be *watching* the scheduled movie(s) at this actual drive-in. When faced with this brand of meddling, parental balderdash it was always wise to be acquainted up front with certain facts, just in case these curious folks were brassy enough to quiz you later. *Cliffs Notes* on B-rated flicks wasn't around yet. So before settling into ". . . a little passionate necking . . . " as Jimmy Stewart called it in the 1947 movie *It's A Wonderful Life*, you had best be alert and remember to eyeball the screen credits as soon as the cameras rolled. Basic film research for most guys simply meant the name and general content of the movie. For an exaggerated instance, consider a movie like *War and Peace*. If my buddies nosy parents asked, "What was the movie about?", the answer would be: Russia. See? Nothing to it . . . off the hook . . . on the "A" list. My mother was never so superficial. I could read her mind. Although she never would admit it, my mother equated any date of mine at a drive-in—inside or outside the car, in the front seat or in the back, with one female or fifty—to be a guaranteed distraction from the regular show and an absolute precursor of subsequent behavior on my part: something akin to the rape and pillage of Sodom and Gomorrah. Her inquisition at breakfast next morning usually resembled a form of Chinese mind torture: "Who was the make-up artist? What was the assistant producer's middle initial? Was it filmed on location? Where was the location?", and finally, "Give me a verbal synopsis of film highlights and 'hum' at least four bars of theme music—key of C, please." I practically had to date a trial lawyer to make it through the interrogation later. With all this pressure, imagine, then, being a minute into the film in the backseat of a '39 Chevy trying to commit some trifling film facts to memory. While struggling for a fleeting glimpse at rolling credits across the screen, my date—this "sweet-young-thing-from-next-door" type, flashing barbed wire for dental braces—had already paralyzed my central nervous system with a vice-like, Ethiopian strangle hold and now hovered over me, poised to collapse both of my lungs with, possibly, her tenth world class lip-lock of the early evening. If you happened to be double dating with a pal and his girl, the situation rapidly became insanity. Imagine the din inside that old jalopy with two times the aforementioned action in progress. (I say "action in progress." It was known as *necking*. Exactly! It comes from the Dark Ages and resembles nothing being done today.) Intense double necking for ten minutes in an airtight '39 Chevy was just about life threatening. It "sealed the tomb," in a sense, leaving enough condensation running off the windows to save on car washes for about a month. The movie sound speakers were normally turned to "low" or "off" during these rituals. After an hour or so of furious, unabated spit-swapping, a sense and period of deep tranquility would usually set in. It was like halftime at the big game, or resting on one's oars. Then, so as to re-adjust body fluids and temperatures, nose-powdering and potty breaks were encouraged and usually observed, followed by the partaking of offered refreshments and other inane bits of nonsense. Once returned to the *tomb* the action was slow to start. Various innocuous small talk passed between the couples. After a tolerable period of observing the civil amenities, the movie resumed and the calm was gradually pierced again as the gasping and groping built to a crescendo until, finally, all hell broke loose and the locker room stench inside that crusty old machine exploded to an eruption of Mount Vesuvian proportions. That fierce onslaught of moaning and groaning and guttural palpitations recalled the agony and death rale of Custer's final stand at Little Big Horn. It portrayed a *reality* the *silver screen* could barely hope to match. Imagine the carnage if you will: four glandularly troubled teen-agers kindled by wild passion—outwardly showing the common symptoms of severe cardiac arrest, with a touch of *St. Vitus's dance* on the side—struggling to survive the night and write yet another chapter in the memorable history of "making out" at the drive-in. Hickies surfaced as the scars of combat. Vehicular implosion was never ruled out. Thank God, the National Anthem played early on. Who could stand straight, or even sit, after such aberrant gymnastics. In those days, on an average date, at the average drive-in lot, enough lips were sealed with enough spit to charge The Hoover Company with copyright infringement in their development of the perfect vacuum.

Another thing these new Hollywood types like to say is "our young actors need real venues to learn their 'craft'." (Another euphemism to prompt instant nausea). Most of these guys weren't even born yet when their so-called *nouveau realite*` was standard fare at every stag party and whore house east of the Pecos. Any guy from my day knows the difference. Back then, being in mixed company meant that a whole different set of rules applied. Sure! Today they call us hypocrites with double standards. If it was a double standard to show respect for some and set an example for others, then, by all means, "Make mine a double!" Furthermore, when we were kids and teenagers, unless you really wanted to get your ass kicked, you never said certain four-letter words in front of girl friends, sisters, mothers or aunts. If by accident you slipped up . . . you were smart to promptly offer apologies all around. Otherwise some muscle bound jock with five hundred varsity letters on his jacket would be instantly dusting the gutter with your lower lip. Believe me, it was tough for some guys. I remember a couple of mangy characters back then who couldn't, or wouldn't, even spell *dog* around a girl without putting "expletive deleted" right between the "d" and the "g". The foreign language students had it best. One guy I knew—with nothing but a "'C' average worth" of ninth grade Latin grammar—used to verbally undress and assault every female he ever met. He strutted like a Roman centurion home on a week-end pass. After he got his initial kicks, he sort of changed into this real sincere and shy character and claimed to be only practicing the Hippocratic Oath for his next career move as a Pre-Med major. The girls usually swooned then with some "oohs" and "aahs" and other phony sounds until his "Latin lover" supercharged ego turned numb and he would move on to dumber pastures. Once, he tried his stunt on a foreign exchange girl from Greece. She understood at once and reported him to the principle. Miss Horndresser honored him immediately with a three day suspension and extra class time in Comparative Languages. Later, with a sly smirk, the Greek lass told friends that any "pre-med jerk" dumb enough to use a phony Latin come-on, then call it a sacred Greek physicians oath, didn't know a *mons pubis* from a "hill on the ground." Almost to a man, though, even the lowest, foulest-mouthed dirtbag in the county knew to clam up like a Trappist monk with lockjaw when females were around expounding on stupid stuff like Friday's dance at the "Y", or "cute" guys, or some other miscellaneous baloney. . . . It was a better time!

Whatever happened to those tender movie scenes of yore . . . films where the man and woman entered a bedroom, then sensuously and slowly closed the door as the camera faded and the screen went dark? The next shot opened to a gorgeous spring morning.

The birds were singing. She was on her bedroom veranda smiling radiantly, arms akimbo, as subtle morning breezes gently massaged her body. Her lover, or husband, or milkman, whoever, was gone-- off to shoot wildebeest in South Philly, or some such place. It was obvious by her each move that between midnight and dawn their ardor had spawned enough celestial energy to send them, *zusammen*, whizzing past Halley's Comet, on the inside track, to the back stretch of the orbit. Now, for the simple memory of that one night stand, she was willing to offer the gods a vow of chastity and spend her remaining days herding yaks in Tibet. Wow! That's when movies sent us a message. There's just one problem with that scene. By modern standards it's too tame. Today it's a laxative commercial.

The typical bedroom scene in modern films is like sitting for extra college credits in descriptive anatomy. Also, can you believe that the "privacy and tenderness" depicted by sex on the screen these days is usually filmed inside a giant studio in front of directors, writers, cameramen, stage hands and a cast of thousands; as well as, most likely, several bus loads of visiting dignitaries from somewhere back East. When we were young teenagers we sarcastically described risqué movies of the day as really mild stuff since nothing was controversial. They only showed the man getting "on and off." Today, film clips of getting on and getting off are considered so bland they're used to preview "coming attractions," even for the so-called G-rated shows—movies once exclusive to Disney as *family fare*. Absolutely nothing is left to the imagination anymore, except that they don't smoke as much after the climax (I mean cigarettes—the industry is committed to a healthier American youth). The highly offensive smoking scene has been traded in for the going-to-the-bathroom shot. Usually a male stud hops out of the sack and heads for the john as the camera zooms for a tight close-up to show our hero relieving himself. The bathroom door is wide open and the sound of urine arching into a pristine bowl is captured forever in living sound and color. These, no doubt, are moments to die for, sending quivers of anticipation through pulsating innards of young Don Juans awaiting a turn at future cinematic glories (Is this *method acting*, or is it still the "fitness America kick" with visuals, demonstrating good prostate health for any geezers watching?). But talk about your reality! This is the true stuff, says Hollywood. . . . Enough of this type of sincerity in your so-called "body of work" (I'm puking again) could easily land you a nomination and have you accepting this year's Oscar from last year's hero, good old "what's-his-name". . . . Gimme a break! Next it'll be amniotic fluid with a twist and slow dancing to peristaltic movements by Al Canal and His Vibrating Tubes. . . . And also, most of us still know to close the door when we go to the bathroom. That's *real* reality.

In my day we were raised on B flicks about war, espionage and westerns . . . didn't care about dialogue or structure. . . . For our dime's worth all we wanted was to see Germans and Japs getting their butts kicked, along with other "just desserts." A sub-plot to us was either a German U-boat movie, or subsidence at the cemetery. We didn't know from subtle emotions to pie-in-the-face. Every spy movie in those days used practically the same actors to play the same characters. We never got enough of them. Just about every movie ever produced during World War II, even the westerns, was about enemy spies stealing American plans for the Norden Bomb Sight, or issuing threats of retaliation toward American relatives still living in Berlin or Tokyo. In Tylertown, the "Old Potato" was the world movie center for westerns and other B flicks. At every Saturday matinee some sinister little guy up on the screen with a phony German accent was grilling your typical all-American good guy: "You haff relatiffs liffing in Ch'ermany still, ja?" Folks around town had lots of German connections. Later, at home, we'd all be wondering about our ancestry and thinking up ways to destroy the evidence.

Getting back to the rotten language they naturally write into scripts these days, the last several generations of Americans were cheated by Hollywood. They never got to enjoy the plain, good old fashioned profanity used early on, when movie standards first loosened. Of course, most everyone remembers *Gone With The Wind* and Clark Gable telling Vivian Leigh that "frankly, he didn't give a damn." But what about some other really dandy expletives such as the "damn and hell" combo—the always impressive dammit-to-hell? Sonofabitch wasn't all that bad—it made an occasional point. For real emphasis, and a little sacrilege on the side, we sometimes heard a few smartly timed "goddammits," and, then, for the grand finale, maybe, one or two thunderous "christ-all-mighties." For maximum results, spacing always helped. A character shouldn't be standing up there spouting fifty curse words per second in one sentence. Spread'em out, I say . . . for a real solid effect. Anything to the contrary sounds gross and really tasteless. Take John Wayne, for instance, or Humphrey Bogart, or even Mae West. They never abused an audience with a diatribe of five thousand obscenities per hour. They could act. Besides, in those days, obscenity in any public forum would have had Police Chief Jack Gillette and the Tylertown *gendarmes* on you like Saran Wrap. Mae West earned her reputation—and bad press (mainly from female and Christian groups)—for being overly suggestive. With a slight hip shimmy and a subtle shift of her extremely brimful *bustenhalter*, she first spoke her famous line to Cary Grant in a 1933 movie called *She Done Him Wrong*: "Come up 'n'. . . see me sometime." Except for Mr. Grant, most of the guys she invited upstairs in later movies were either too old or too drunk to make the first three steps. Imagine a modern rendition of that scene: Today's ingenue`, after trying to determine her motivation—or, better yet, what is motivation?— would naturally substitute body action for emotion. The "tease" is a lost art, so ultimately the action would center on a pile of fibrillating, sweaty flesh humping away somewhere "amid the tasteful ambience and quiet seclusion" of say, center stage at the Festival of San Fermin in Pamplona, Spain, during a running of the bulls. Hollywood, with its infinite precocity, would probably think up a new Oscar category and give it the nod for "Best portrayal of sex in a religious setting." This would naturally open the door for the Foreign Film Festival guys and their award for "Most elegant use of sex and religion at a sporting event." Regardless, the bottom line is: Given today's rock bottom standards, every movie maker around wants credit for the dirtiest, raunchiest story that mankind can concoct. So much for reviving The Legion of Decency.

Most folks I knew in the old days happily "escaped" reality for the sanctuary of the local movie house. Not that reality was oppressive, but in the 40s and 50s a motion picture at a fair price was always welcome fantasy . . . the stuff of dreams. Every schoolboy knew that after spending his hard earned eleven cents to watch a cartoon, a weekly serial and the best B flick Hollywood had in the vault, reality—good or bad—like an "aromatic" breeze from the local Tylertown paper mill, would faithfully rap you smack in the kisser the very moment your feet left the "Old Potato" and shoe leather hit the pavement outside on Pennsylvania Avenue.

Chapter Nine

Religion

Graceland Gazette, Memphis, TN, August 12, 3001:
Once again the world religious community anxiously awaits August 16th. The sacred city at Graceland, diocese of the Most Holy Apostolic Presleyan Heartbreak Hotel & Church of America, Tennessee Synod, expects record crowds this week for the holy pilgrimage to the shrine of Elvis Presley of Tupelo. At this annual observance of Rockabilly Requiem millions of devout worshipers will celebrate the 1,024th anniversary of His death and promised resurrection. Presley of Tupelo—Christ to the civilized world's three billion Presleyans—will be praised throughout the week in continuous sacred services conducted from within the walls of the Holy See at Graceland. Church leaders will stress a "unity in trinity" approach to the faithful as they seek fellowship with their own, as well as non-Presleyans, through their ancient credo: *Treat Me Nice, Love Me Tender and Don't Be Cruel.* At Graceland's Hound Dog Gardens, the procession of the Kissing of the Blue Suede Shoes will be ongo-

ing at His shrine throughout the day and night—regardless of weather—until all attending validated worshippers can be accommodated at His throne. Worshipers holding a current year "Christ! I think I saw Elvis" card are requested to gather each morning at sunrise and partake *en masse* in the groveling at His shrine. Also during the sunrise festivities, a solemn service will be conducted using responsive readings from the Prayer Book of the Righteous Reverend Colonel Thomas of Parker, along with selected hymns offered by the Lawdy, Miss Clawdy Acappella Choir for Genteel Southern Voices. During the week formal services will be conducted inside the Crying in the Chapel Chapel. Seating will be assigned as available. Those Presleyans holding officially consecrated, life member "I Really Saw Elvis" cards may proceed immediately to the front of the chapel to share in the wailing undulations at the waters of the Let's Have A Party Pool. The annual telling of His death—*Return to Sender*—and His resurrection—*Good Rockin' Tonight*—will be presented by the nuns of the Holy Order of the Virgin Priscilla Convent of the Little Sister. A musical program will be presented by the Chapel Mixed Choir, with soloist, Saint Roy of Orbison impersonator, Dover Dykes, dubbing the voice of Him in a rendition of *A Big Hunk O' Love*. The internationally renowned Graceland Instrumental Quartet will perform the offertory music, playing *Money Honey* in the passe` style of ancient Nashvillian Brassists. The daily recessional will be highlighted by a primitive "slow shuffle" rendition of *Loving You*, sung in unison *a la* the archaic French Quarter Scrolls interpretation of the antediluvian New Orleans Delta Era tribal tunes (not to be confused with last year's lunar tunes of the Crescent Era). Upon departure from the chapel, all worshipers in reasonably good health are urged to "do your best for Him" while executing the "Presleyan pelvic gyration."

Light refreshments will be served throughout the week in the Jailhouse Rock Hall. Contribution of edibles by guests is most sincerely welcome. No low-fat, low-cal, or low-salt dishes, please. A vast array of wholesome foods will be available at all hours, consisting of fried meats and sausages, French fried potatoes and onion rings, buttery mashed potatoes, possum fat gravy, assorted cheeses, pies, cakes, eclairs, chocolate bon bons and, for the elderly and infirm, an assortment of unctuous puddings. Beer and other alcoholic beverages will be available only as part of Communion services each evening. Please have ID's available. Children under two not admitted without proper DNA mapping.

Each year the Rockabilly Requiem celebration at Graceland exceeds itself in pious excellence as it marks the conclusion of the religious year for the world's growing fellowship of Orthodox Presleyans. The next major event on the church calendar will be Holy Presleymas on January 8, 3002, the 1,067th anniversary of the King's birth into common poverty on the knotty pine sidebar of a Tupelo, Mississippi honky tonk in the year 1935.

Welcome back.

Senior citizenry gives me a different slant on the religion I knew and practiced as a lad and teenager. It's not that religion has changed. The change is in "religious" people and the things they do, or don't condone. ". . . *and a child shall lead them.*" What if a thirteen year old computer whiz accidentally discovered that www.JC@heav.GOD was the web site of Jesus Christ? And suppose in an E-mail message to this kid, Jesus spoke of his "second coming" during the next Easter season and directed the lad to spread the Word. On the surface, nothing much would happen directly . . . . Oh, the kid would be whisked off, *stat*, to a padded cell in Bellview for tests and signs of congenital brain damage; the Feds would probably trash his computer searching for a Chinese or Middle East connection; and, as a last resort, he would, no doubt, be branded a hard core reactionary and ploy of the religious right. The real fun, however, would come on the next Good Friday when a clean-shaven Jesus Christ deplaned at New York's JFK Airport wearing a madras jacket and Nike sneakers and the initials IHS on his carry-on luggage. S.W.A.T teams would be on the tarmac "at the ready," with national guardsmen and state police "on hold" inside the terminal. At the first sign of a salutation or sign of the Cross, the Son of God would be beaten senseless, chained like an animal and held over for district night court. Within eight hours he'd be charged with subversive acts and, subsequently, "lost" somewhere inside the Rikers Island compound with nary a chance of bail in sight. We, as a society, would be looking for some vast conspiracy behind his actions and trying like hell to lay blame on the political system, or welfare system, or any other system appearing ripe for an official "comeuppance."

In the old days we'd flat out call it a hoax . . . but a nice, friendly, fuzzy hoax. We'd even have some fun with it . . . give it the benefit of the doubt . . . maybe have "Him" talk at some Rotary luncheons, or maybe even a joint session of Congress (we let General MacArthur speak there in 1951. He brought down the house. Most of the country actually thought he *was* God). In the forties and fifties such foolishness became a human interest gem. Now—since the world has gotten a lethal taste of "going to hell in a hand cart"—it's legitimately a terrorist threat or an alien conspiracy.

I'm jaded, I know, but the entire religious experience used to refresh body, mind and spirit. For some, I'm sure, it still does. Long ago, the direct line within family, school and church was perceptible, profound and connected. In forty years that line has traveled from the ramrod backbone of our national pride to socialistic curvature of the spine. The slightest perceived overlap these days between church and state instantly launches your average liberal nitwit into a frothing conniption and knee jerk call to his or her nearest ACLU fanatic. Political hacks have been ordaining morality out of our lives for decades. With the same rule-of-thumb agendas and mindless overkill, they seem never to consider that their legislative tampering ultimately destroys a proud timeline of traditional values. Each new law effectively donates entitlement to some and pervasive inequity to others. When to stop fixing things that were never broken, is the question, as well as admitting to the base corruption in politics and politicians. This path has been traveled before—in other times, other civilizations. How far must it now go before some perfectly sane world statesman-types step forward to scream "Stop! It's nuts! It won't work this time, either!" For certain, more damage is coming before help is on the way. Except for world missionary work, organized religion in America has not fought the good fight against the moral dry rot of the legislative process. *Religious America* has not countered well . . . has not pervaded anything. 'Tis a pity to think . . . maybe we've not let it. More and more over the years the Christian bible has become a literal document—dispossessed of life, breath and change—devoid of symbolism and practicality. . . . *If it ain't like it says, it ain't.*

Possibly it's a fancy of youth but in the forties and fifties we, as a nation, blithely displayed our trust and faith in a higher power. During our heyday the sense of right and wrong, black and white always seemed clearer, though temptation then was no different than today. Self-esteem was big. We had a healthy belief in ourselves. Some of us learned that "every hair makes its shadow on the ground."[23] Perhaps, to our good fortune, we oversimplified the system. But what's really to complicate? What made the change? It seems folks now accept values infinitely more diverse and obtuse for no other reason than to justify a random thought or deed. Society accepts a wide range of divergent behavior these days. Again, most has been legislated. It's simply to say: Everything we think and do is okay.

Who are the role models today? How do we manage the gray areas, if we even see them? Is it right or wrong . . . acceptance or denial? What are the standards? Do we have standards? The same old question pops up: How did we get from there to here . . . and where do we go now, from here? So I ask: What's it to be in year 3000? Do we continue to denigrate our forefather's lessons of common morality? The canonization of "Elvis the pelvis" during the twenty-first century is certainly nonsense and quite absurd. But what's to prevent it? Our religious leaders aren't exactly being showered with "high fives" these days. Religion as we knew it years ago has a dilemma. Maybe it's simply about the message of religion, and the capabilities of religious people at "marketing" the Word of God in these *sophisticated* days. Perhaps it reflects fatigue in these modern times with worn-out routines: Do as I say, not as I do. . . . Show and tell (confession). . . . Meaningless ritual. . . . Ceremony. . . . Change for change's sake. . . . Boring?" It's a fact that a few churches today actually "interview" prospective candidates for membership. It's worse than joining a country club: Name at least three (3) known church members in good standing; provide a bank and three (3) retail credit references; give us a salary history, educational background, church giving habits, D & B rating, tax bracket, blood type, golf handicap, and would you be willing for the Church to have power of attorney at the reading of your Last Will and Testament? Heaven forbid you should die a pauper or have "no-account" relatives active in the Salvation Army. Floridians elect presidents easier than this.

And why do conventional church people still obsess with the preference that pious words and long, somber faces come first in God's Kingdom? Is curiosity and common sense about God out of style? Have we let His supposed aura and power overwhelm us? A "home remedy" for this malaise is a *treatment* at which we're all experts: *Think of yourself first*. Think of yourself strictly in the "heaven of here and now," not in that other one at " hereafter and beyond." As "piano man" Billy Joel says:

>"Who needs a house out in Hackensack?
>Is that what you get with your money?
>It seems such a waste of time,
>If that's what it's all about,
>If that's movin' up then I'm movin' out."[24]

Faith and good works is the key. And that doesn't mean always rolling your eyes like some damn idiotic mesmerizer, or being a gratuitous bore—forever spewing some "sermon-on-the-mount-type" recitation at the first sound of a discouraging word. And, unless asked, don't be one of those self-justifying, humanity pestering boobs that can't help from spouting bible chapter and verse for every perceived miscarriage of humanity, and bragging all about how you've been "born again" and the rest of us poor slobs are doomed to eternal damnation if we just happen to be so lucky. Remember the key—faith and good works! Get with the real program! It's not about *you* somewhere off in some gold-lined heaven. It's about *your* idea of that heaven, right now—right here on earth, at your job, in your school, on your street, in your backyard, in your shack, or at your estate . . . for *you and all you touch*.

If reincarnation does exist, then, certain assholes out there should really brace for an unholy *force majeure*. We all know them, too. Most importantly, we know for sure they are not us . . . absolutely not! The ones we really indict are those Sunday souls with legacies forged from a lifetime of giving particular hell to the human race in general—the so-called "no nonsense" types who would eat dust rather than act out a kindness, yet beg even the silence for the faintest praise—the ones shouting "do unto others as you would do unto others" and then expect a stretch limo for that hallowed jaunt to the great beyond. Surely these folks will have long faces someday if, after an *exemplary* life and a *sovereign's* funeral, they're reborn into some planetary complex where their skin is dark and from dawn to dusk they move over the fields picking a flower called "cotton" in a place called the South, having to wander the system again and again through the eternity of time until, in some future eon, they may possibly get it right.

Since time began it was, and is, a long haul and a tough road from birth to death. A helping hand never hurts. It always helps.

Chapter Ten

Sports

During the 1940s and 1950s—my personal sacred days of yore—a classic *frontispiece* to American athletics was college football and the idyllic Homecoming Weekend celebration. Cast in a dream setting of a warm, golden Saturday in October, the occasion usually played out 'midst falling leaves, flasks of "Guzzler's Gin,"[25] and variously laden "spreads" of tailgate cuisine. The "big game," and the chaotic, saturating noise of band music and cheerleaders surrounding it, became the immediate thing and everything. Authentic Americana demanded that *football* be center stage and that the game should go down to the wire—one more for the Gipper—against the longest odds known to the western world. As any freshman knew, slightly less momentous than "the game" was "at the game," showing the guys and other skeptics a rakish jaunt to stadium seats with a fair campus lass at your side and, thus, at your command. No matter her bearing, girth, complexion or credentials—whether Prom Queen, Sorority Queen, or a mere bespectacled "drudge" from the Student Union crowd—the time-honored Homecoming gala beckoned each frosh and upper classman to the significant task of procuring a warm body (preferably opposite sex) for the solemn week-end of unforgettable moment yet to unfold, noteworthy events predicted to occupy the mind's eye for decades to come, barring mental blind spots later in life when reputation and image building take hold. Prior to such majestic Homecoming pomp, the campus underground had usually leaked enough subtle "asides" around school to inspire even the dullest red-blooded student to arrange for "company" of his (or her) own liking, upon which—if so inspired—to throw caution aside and pledge one's solemn troth, i.e., "a promise to cherish 'til death, expulsion, final exams, or pending draft notice, do we part." Homecoming hype after the game is what it was really about and was never taken lightly. Each couple's mutually expressed platitudes toward one another were intended to dove-tail precisely with the exchanging of rings and pins against a backdrop of Old Main towering high above sturdy oaks as the soft, acappella sounds of "Sweetheart of Sigma Chi" echoed on a wafting breeze.

This, at least, was how it *seemed* to read between the lines of the college grapevine. Those communiqués never did mention that an average campus "queen" was as scarce as clean underwear. Every pretty girl in Happy Valley practically had her pick of the entire campus. These gals, I think, chose "dates" by a select lottery system, i.e., from ballots submitted exclusively by athletes with intricate interlocking fraternity connections. Naturally, that left us non-pedigreed, Student Union creeps to troll the streets of State College, PA for town girls (a definite plus, I might add, both economically and festively). Meanwhile, back on campus, the queens exercised their options with every athletic discipline and frat house in town. Further complicating the dating scheme was that your typical queen was seldom content with "honey" from a single hive. A few I remember at Penn State looked for "hunks"—usually the football variety—from any college within the confines of the continental United States and Canada, including Territories and Dependencies. It was a conquest thing, as they say today. One girl's telephone became known as the "international date line." Her phone bill, no doubt, resembled a United Nations networking scheme. She was reminiscent of an old song:

>"She's got a halfback at California,
>She loves a quarterback at Notre Dame,
>She threw a tackle at Alabama,
>And a Fordham guard's her flame,
>She goes to "proms" with an Army fullback,
>A Navy center has her in a whirl,
>She's got a sweetheart at every college,
>She's just an All-American girl!"[26]

Foggy memories of 1951 and 1952 remind me that unless one was a brilliant student, jock or frat member, freshman year was a drag. I was none of the above as I worked my butt off trying to pay my own way. There wasn't a scholarship or GI Bill in sight.

Hazing by upperclassmen was harmless. Returning World War II veterans in the upper classes took the edge and meanness out of, what ended up as being, infantile pranks. Football pep rallies were fun. Joe Paterno had just joined Coach Rip Engle's staff as quarterback coach that year. He was introduced at a pep rally one Friday night where, for about a nano second, I met him face to face. I wonder if Joe remembers?

I harbored no aspirations to play sports at Penn State. Given my anemic size at the time, I certainly wasn't about to be a football walk-on with scholarship players like Lenny Moore around. My experience as a high school player had been a plethora of: "What if's . . . ." and "It might have been, if . . . ." With a smattering of experience behind me—*smattering* is French for "practically none"—I tried out for State's freshman lacrosse team. I soon found that competing against scholarship players and high school stars wasn't a cake walk in any sport. Reluctantly, my Penn State athletic career ended. Nothing was working at that early time in my life. It reminded me of first experiences learning to play baseball, which, in turn, reminded me of "Penn State baseball" in the spring. . . . I was heartened. Baseball could be my ticket. . . . Lucky for me, or lucky for Penn State baseball . . . it never happened.

At Cahill Sports Center in Baltimore, MD in 1945, I was the runt of the litter where baseball was concerned. I played right field on the Cahill team. At age twelve I practically needed a cross-town trolley and two transfers to reach my outfield "outpost" before the action started. As kids, the youngest, or worst, guy on any baseball team—I was both—got to "play" in right field. It makes perfect sense now. It was a vast wasteland out there in right—hardly any action. Why let a twelve year old kid screw up a perfectly good ball game? Stick 'im in right. At the age of innocence, what kid knew about switch hitting, hit and run, or run and hit strategies? What kid understood *strategy?* What kid could pronounce it? Besides, as I recall, back then natural "lefty" batters were either total strike-out artists or non-existent. So with only a few hits coming in my direction during the season, I could've been parking cars and making a buck or two. I didn't need a strong arm to play right field. This was fortunate since my throwing arm performed with the agility of a limp noodle on novocaine. When I first started playing baseball, on a throw back to the infield they'd tell me to "hit the cut-off man." At first I thought the cut-off man was this little midget-of-a guy we used for an umpire and who hung around second base. Most of the time, however, there was nothing to throw back.

My parents were too poor in those days for me to have a real store-bought glove like the other guys. Besides, I was too small and still growing. Usually I had to borrow the raggiest piece of regulation junk that somebody was willing to part with for the duration of the game. As a result, my "on field" mitt made my left arm and hand look like a skinny, little upright gizmo, balancing a giant cow patty at the top end. Given the condition and stench of the glove, a real cow patty would've given me a fresh air "high" since during the game my left hand usually smelled like road-kill held over from the *dog days* of summer. Most of the time my glove fit like a bushel basket. At rare moments that circumstance did a "180 flip."

Occasionally some lucky, unconscious batter connected on a late swing, thus launching—to my absolute terror— a rare fly ball in the general direction of the five acres of freshly plowed pasture I seemed to be covering in right field. At such times, to my remembered misery, my glove hand instantly mutated from a colossal *cow turd* to a shrink-wrapped *petri dish*. Trying to catch a high fly ball in Herr Petri's dish was like maneuvering under a solitary Spanish peanut in a wind tunnel. Meanwhile, under my feet, some random, impromptu, earthquake-like tremor was just starting to register nine-point-zero on the Richter Scale. As the falling baseball re-entered the earth's atmosphere and I struggled for position precisely underneath, I must've resembled a road runner at top speed in hot tar. I used to shout, " I got it! I got it!" Then I looked down at my glove: "I don't got it." Some comedian somewhere uses that routine in a comedy act. Well, he stole it from me. In 1945 I invented those lines to get me through tough ball games.... It didn't help. It may be a comic's routine today ... but I was the original "comic." I was a solo act. And I never thought it was so damn funny. Not to worry, though. As the regular right fielder, I only faced sweeping condemnation and humiliation about once in every three or four ballgames.

Some may wonder why I was never benched. Simple! ... I could hit. It would be years until the "designated hitter rule"—a *liberal entitlement device*, no doubt—was conceived and allowed by major league baseball. As the youngest, smallest kid on the team I regularly got on base with the best of them. I could hit fast balls, slow balls and "stuff," if any pitcher had any and was able to control it. A curve ball or change-up was rare at our young level of play. Some sorry saps used to obsess in their own pitching skill by throwing something called a "drop"—a forerunner of the slider, I think. No young pitcher could control it (hands too small). But they kept throwing it, one time after another. At bat, many times all I did was to wait out four misguided "drops" and move to first base. It was practically an intentional walk. My specialty in those years was the bunt. I lusted to be at bat with a man on third and a squeeze play called. To lay down a perfect bunt on the "suicide squeeze" was, for me, easier than brushing my teeth in the dark. It was all *touch*. When the ball hit the head of my limp bat, relaxed hands did the rest and scored the run—a cinch at any level.

Practically every facet of youth-oriented athletic activity from the 1940s is a mere memory today to any geezer still alive and old enough to recall. There's absolutely nothing around today that compares with the simplicity and innocence of that era's sport scene. I worry that our old ways: the random, corner lot pick-up game; or back alley basketball; or middle-of-the-street touch football; are things of the past—gone and forgotten. Kids don't seem to play just for the fun of it anymore. In fact, most don't play anything without uniforms and "five thousand dollar" shoes. The shoes of today would've made a guy in my era the laughing stock of the county— justly qualified to be chased back home for *proper* footwear, something mangy and recognizable. Now, everything's a means to an end. When we played around the neighborhood in the old days, my parents weren't on the sidelines cheering me on. As long as we were happy at play and not stealing cars or robbing banks, they were happy. Parents today are involved in everything when it comes to guiding little Johnny on the road toward sport's riches and fame— from step one and day one. These kids have personal trainers and motivators. There are strength coaches and, no doubt, financial advisors for the inevitable day when . . . the "big time" comes to call. Some use agents and sponsors and business managers. It's not unusual for all of these jobs to be concentrated into a single entity: The Family Sports Complex run by President Dad and Vice President Mom.

Females are in the mix, big time, these days. In my time all but a handful of girls showed a strong inclination toward an athletic career. They were limited to golf and tennis, track and field, skating or swimming. Women's basketball rules and uniforms were pitiful and confining, enough so to make the actual playing of the game laughable. It was like watching a bunch of cloistered nuns play dodge ball. There was a dubious theory expounded during my youth that young, teen-age girls had been content growing up with dolls and jump ropes and junior high dances until discovering that young, teen-age male athletes wore a certain, required item of gear—whispered about in secret cliques—called an athletic supporter. Instantly female interest in male sport's games soared: "What's it look like? What's it for? It supports . . . *what*!" Teen-age girls, naturally, were drawn to young athletes of their liking. They started hanging around the practice facilities and boy's locker rooms, curious to overhear guy-talk about "inside" stuff. Donning that first supporter, I suppose, was like a girl strapping on her first brassiere. Personally, I never remembered my first athletic supporter as an "occasion," or even a Kodak moment, other than to think: "Don't these things come any smaller?" But young school girls were exposing a first, curious interest in things athletic, not the least of which was a chance to share with friends secret thoughts of sweaty jocks and their straps. Women eventually got their own unique piece of equipment in the "sports bra," although most NFL linemen could've easily qualified to wear both. Like condoms, athletic supporters were once sold semi-secretly—in sporting goods stores, behind and beneath the counter. They were well disguised. If you'd bought a top of the line supporter not knowing it was made by Bike, later at the YMCA gym you'd possibly be expecting to pull a sprocket chain from the box. The athletic supporter was a treasured item of male sports gear. An unmentionable—like ladies undies—now it's bandied about and described in mixed company, at parties and dances, to a fair-thee-well. Some old timers may wonder: *Is nothing sacred anymore?* By modern standards that's a bit too prudish for a piece of equipment that, over time, has become run-of-the-mill. As sports memorabilia goes, mixed company today freely calls it a "jock strap." Such a description offends language purists who know that *jock* is a Scottish derivation of Jack, as well as an 1895 slang term for penis. Still, others are offended since it suggests a connotation of sweaty, smelly crotches. Why not a clinical, one-size-fits-all approach (no pun intended)? Call it what it is—a *penis protector*—and get on with life. Generally, nothing is too gross for mixed company anymore, not even talk about cruddy jock straps, unwashed for about four years, harboring every fungus this side of China, and smelling like hundred-year old eggs before petrifaction. It's a given that certain athletes will dress for practice or a game by replacing clean clothes for a dirty jock, socks and undershirt. In the sport's milieu, some facts are set in stone. There's a perfect explanation. Athletes are super, superstitious and heartily believe: "If it ain't broke, don't fix it." In other words: "Never change your socks or jocks in the middle of a winning season." By default, then, certain things at certain times are expected to smell like a sweaty crotch.

In the summer of 1949 I played American Legion ball in Tylertown as an outfielder and reserve catcher. One hot afternoon in July we were to play the second game of a scheduled doubleheader. Most of our starters were banged up from the first game. I was scheduled to catch the second game. Donny Wells, a skinny, bookish type kid who should have been the batboy, was our only healthy pitcher—a relief pitcher, at that. In actual fact, Donny had never thrown *a pitch*, in *a game*, in his young life. He had talked his way onto the team. He was a sports memorabilia nut— a *maven*, of sorts, the Howard Cosell of his day. After an impromptu, pre-season chat with Coach Lapore—I think Coach figured by some fluke he'd discovered a budding Cy Young—Donny was asked to join the team. Though he could talk like a throwback from the '27 New York Yankees, I knew Donny to be a fraud. He couldn't pitch. His arm was absolutely puny. Sometimes, during practice, to pass the time, I used to "warm him up." He had one hellish imagination. One day he would be Dizzy Dean, the next, Spud Chandler, or Hal Newhouser, and making like he was throwing "spitters" and sliders and big, old round-house curves—like it was World Series, seventh game, bottom of the ninth, two outs, three and two count, bases loaded. Mentally, he always was on the mound protecting a one-run lead, going into his final motion for a pitch to the slouching Babe Ruth, waiting in the batter's box with his fifty-five pound bat cocked behind his ear, ready to send Donny's closing pitch into orbit. Naturally . . . the Babe always struck out. Oddly enough—in real life—Donny could actually, consistently throw a sweeping curve ball and make it break across the plate. On his best day, however, the ball traveled about *one* mile an hour and hardly made a dent in the catcher's mitt. Long story short: That afternoon Coach Lapore started Donny against a team from *down in the country* somewhere, with players the size of mature gorillas, using bats the size of small trees. Donny was petrified. His immediate challenge was to retain his own body fluids. Coach told me to work with him: "Keep 'im fresh. Talk to 'im. Keep the ball down. We got seven players behind 'im." I went out to the mound. "Donny, ya got one pitch. Give it lotsa' motion an' keep it comin'. Mebbe we'll get lucky."

The game went seven innings. We won, 3 to 2. They got their only runs from a hit with men on base, a passed ball and a wild pitch. The wild pitch wasn't really "wild"—the ball lost momentum about ten feet in front of the plate and rolled dead. As I mentioned, in those days young ball players rarely faced a curve ball pitcher. It's a fact that hasn't drastically changed. From the instant of Donny's very first round-house curve—no matter, slow, slower, slowest—he had those *apes* swinging and hopping around like "jive jockeys" at a Benny Goodman dance marathon. He won his only game with a one-pitch repertoire. That sweeping curve had them vacating the batter's box at least six different ways. Every couple of innings Coach took me aside and complimented the way I was handling him. Handling, nothing! I never told Coach that our arsenal only contained one pitch. Assuming we even had a fast ball that could've reached the batter's box, it was guaranteed to be slammed straight into upstate New York. Around the fifth inning Donny walked off the mound. I went out to him. He had a tear in his eye. He said his arm was sore. I urged him to finish. At game's end—after we won—jubilant team members celebrated and carried Donny around the field. Later, Coach Lapore slapped me on the back: "Ya called a great game." It wasn't so great. Donny's tears as he was hoisted on shoulders and carried aloft were tears of pain, not joy. As for calling a great game: The guy only had one pitch to throw. Lucky for Donny, those guys never even got a lucky hit. Sadly, Donny had consumed his baseball career in a single afternoon. He never finished the season. He never pitched or tried to pitch again. Pity not, though. Donny Wells was an academic wizard and made a gazillion bucks from a better-than-average I.Q. and acceptance in marriage by a legitimate Tylertown *queen*. Today he enjoys the posh life somewhere in a gated Florida retirement community—I think—and likely recalls a *round house curve* to be an interior dimension of his domed, backyard arboretum.

I left Penn State in 1952 for the Navy. After discharge I got married and enrolled at an all-male school. At last, the problem of available campus females was solved. The Korean War was behind and school on the GI Bill lay ahead.

After looking to the past from today's vantage point, sadly I concluded: Forget about 1950s college football and Homecoming Weekends. The new American sports scene projects a stark and different face. Today the number one sports game in town is marketing. There is no athletic contest in the world that fails to attract an audience. With an audience comes demand. With demand comes the exploitation of everything possible to produce income. Athletic endeavor has become a major industry. It was proven in 1981 when a seven-week strike by the Major League Baseball Players Association caused the cancellation of 713 regular season games. Financial loss in player's salaries and television revenues was staggering. Organized labor and collective bargaining had discovered a home in professional sports. It was a fact further enforced in 1987 during a 24-day strike by the National Football League Players Association. By the late 1980's the sports industry in the United States alone was a fifty billion dollar business. Television was, and is, the most obvious part of the industry. In addition, consider the millions of dollars involved with retailing of sports equipment and clothing; construction and maintenance of stadiums, health clubs, golf courses, tennis courts, race tracks, bowling alleys, skating rinks; sales of food and drink at events; salaries of announcers and columnists; agents, lawyers, and managers for athletes; product endorsements by athletes, sports medicine, and sports insurance. Don't forget corporate sponsorship of everything from "bat day" and "camera day" at baseball games to football's "pass, punt and kick" contests. Even some tailgate parties have corporate sponsors. Corporations underwrite major sporting events these days on a gargantuan scale. A traditional New Year's Day in America used to feature four or five traditional bowl championship games. It's a practice gone by the boards. There are now enough corporate sponsored bowl games on television to occupy the family from December 26th through the first week in January. Among others, we now play the Tostito Fiesta Bowl, Nokia Sugar Bowl, Toyota Gator Bowl, Capital One Citrus Bowl, Outback Bowl, Alamo Bowl, FedEx Orange Bowl. (What, no Mulligan's Meatless Meatballs No-Beef Bowl?) The grand daddy of them all—for now, at least—is still the Rose Bowl, except now it's the AT&T Rose Bowl and played four days after New Year's Day, supposedly for the national championship, but really for TV ratings since it's the only game being televised on that particular night in early January. Corporations are even paying to have their names on new stadiums being built. Cases in point: Invesco Field - Denver; Alltel Stadium - Jacksonville; RCA Dome - Indianapolis; Heinz Field - Pittsburgh, to name a few. With the recent profile of major corporations in bankruptcy, it may stop.

Professional athletes today are among the highest paid people in the world. Athletes are celebrities in their chosen sport, as much so as movie and television stars. Athletics has trumped *academia*. Talented athletes, urged on by family and friends, choose to leave college—sometimes high school—early these days to be drafted by major sports organizations. They pursue specialized physical regimens fanatically. Boys and girls begin training as early as five or six years old to be ready in the future for their introduction to success and the big bucks out there. All major professional sport teams participate in some form of organized farm system—most notably baseball—or working relationships with certain schools. In the last fifty years growth in these systems has been phenomenal. By far, the major impetus to that growth has been the spread of television. Television provides instant visibility. But TV's real power over sports is money. Money from commercial sponsors who buy broadcast time from the networks, with the networks then paying the professional leagues or others for the right to broadcast the events. Sadly, only a small percentage of young athletes can ever hope to attain professional status, and an even smaller number will ever gain "superstar" levels. Most participants are driven by money and perks. On the downside for prospective superstars is that early devotion to their sports careers often has had serious side effects. Extreme pressure from parents and coaches can be psychologically devastating in young athletes. There's the danger of early disabling accidents. Grade schoolers—as earlier mentioned—being forced or allowed to emulate major league pitchers, run the risk of permanent arm damage. Emphasis on athletics over academics has sent more than one former superstar to the unemployment line. This is where academic-minded coaches like Joe Paterno excel off the field as well as on. Most often when a young, uneducated athlete fails, there's nothing much but, "It might have been!" on which to fall back.[27]

In the "lah-dee-dah" arena of modern pro football elitists, the original National Football League owners from the 1920s and 1930s were, in my opinion, strictly "blue collar" types. A few of their teams still are. Consider the Green Bay Packers, Chicago Bears, New York Giants, and Pittsburgh Steelers. Although business is forever business, and profit is the reason to be in business, it's difficult to imagine owners Curly Lambeau, George Halas, Tim Mara, and Art Rooney, as anything less than dedicated football pioneers. Mr. Rooney, a gentleman in every sense of the word, was always my role model. The Rooney family today still conducts business by the ethical principles of their founding father. Mr. Rooney and I had something in common: Late in the 1972 football season, toward the end of an apparent losing effort by the Steelers against the Oakland Raiders, Mr. Rooney and I both decided to put the loss behind us and headed toward our individual bathrooms—Mr. Rooney at Three Rivers Stadium, me at my home in Greensburg, PA. We both missed Franco Harris' "immaculate reception" of Terry Bradshaw's deflected pass that scored a touchdown and won the game for Pittsburgh. Many Pittsburghers swear that that play was a sign from the "football gods" foretelling of the great Steeler teams to come.

Athletes are different today. Individually, many stand out. As a group they are a bunch of angry people with too much money and time to spend. Some display a demeanor that is foul and unattractive. Kids have fewer role models in sports today. Where is the next Arnold Palmer, Joe Green, Babe Didrikson, John Unitas, Lynn Swann, Tom Landry, Gayle Sayers, Wilma Rudolph, Tiger Woods, Jack Nicklaus, Bob Feller, Danny Murtaugh, Jesse Owens, Bob Richards, Stan Musial, Roy Campanella, Yogi Berra, Bill Russell, Vince Lombardi, David Robinson, Joe Louis, Roger Staubach, Terry Bradshaw, Jerry Rice, Nancy Lopez, Peggy Fleming, Arthur Ashe, Hank Aaron, Don Budge, Joe DiMaggio, Chris Evert, Lou Gehrig, Ben Hogan, Jackie Joyner-Kersee, Sandy Koufax, Bill Walsh, Knute Rockne, Vernon Law, George Gipp, Casey Stengel, Bill Mazerowski, Chuck Noll, Jim Thorpe, Helen Wills Moody, George Halas? These kinds aren't turning up as frequently anymore. Everything is driven by the money. So few athletes, it appears these days, take time to express publicly their gratitude and responsibility as role models. Athletes of at least one sport are around us all, all the time. Imagine, then, the effect on our youth from a total, concerted effort by sport players at all levels to "live their image" day by day in a positive, constructive way. Imagine that the games were once for the exchange of a pin or a trophy; then it was cars, clothes and vacations; today "stars" are barely happy with a mere beer distributorship, or Coca Cola franchise, or a couple McDonald's restaurants. With a certain handful of "superstars" it's become a game of "Who can top this?" They want money—millions and millions in salary and bonus and perks—and put it all in a lifetime contract. Contractual bonus payouts exist in an ever increasing multitude of player performance categories: touchdown catches, rushing yards, touchdown passes, runs batted in, earned run average. The list is endless. The list will continue to grow before agents, players and owners return to sanity. I can imagine them negotiating extra bonus for things like: sitting up straight at team meetings, the ability to limit end zone showboating to under five minutes, staying awake while sitting up straight at team meetings, keeping basketball rim hang time down to a minute, etc., etc.

Again, looking back, the old times were best. Even our legal system "caved" to the civil libertarians and altered the rules of golf so to accommodate individual deficiencies. Speaking of golf, allow me to digress—

How is it that pro golfers can chunk a ball into the rough and immediately find it lying on a cart path, or on top of a pile of debris at an angle directly facing the hole, or on the back of a turtle heading straight for the green? When my ball lands in the rough, I need to call out the National Guard or a team of mining engineers. My treks to the woods are like safaris to deepest Africa in search of rare jewels or the long, lost Judge Crater.

Back to subject—

The U. S. Supreme Court recently ruled in favor of pro golfer Casey Martin under the Americans With Disabilities Act stating that they (the Court) knew that Martin endured excessive fatigue during golf tournaments due to walking with a degenerative leg condition. Such disability—they judged—should allow him the use of a golf cart during professional tournaments. Furthermore, regular walking by non-handicapped players only causes regular fatigue, and regular walking is not "fundamental to such competition"—this last epiphany coming from such eminent scratch golfers as Justice Stevens, Rehnquist, Ginsburg, *et al.* Well, Ben Hogan—rest his soul—is doing a 180 roll.

In 1949, Hogan was all but pronounced dead from a head-on highway collision. His pelvis and shoulder were crushed, his leg and ankle broken. He applied for the U.S.Open from his hospital bed. Hogan entered the 1950 U.S.Open—sixteen months after being told he would never walk again—and won. The next year he won a third U.S.Open and his first Masters. Hogan came back to the game without a whimper, neither asking for a cart or a cane and probably not even orthopedic shoes. Once, when asked his secret for winning golf, Hogan replied, "Finish with the lowest score."

The highest court in the land has now liberalized and opened the door for even further abuse. I can see it now: In coming years every marginal-to-mediocre golfer in the land will have his or her PGA card and be crisscrossing American golf courses *ad nauseam* in souped up, pin striped, banner waving carts with caddy side seats making like rubber bumper cars at Hershey Park. On the event of the first mid-course collision the cry will go forth to establish Federal Traffic Regulations for all PGA Golf Courses—rights of way; radar controlled speeds on cart paths; dimmed headlights and blinking hazard lights for inclement weather, etc. Then it'll be seat belts and air bags, and surround-around cart screening for errant balls in flight. Eventually, certain soggy and marshy course areas will catch the eye of whacko environmentalists posing as golf fans and, in time, by federal statute, be declared non-retrievable lies, as well as impassable, impenetrable wetlands subject to fines and jail time if trespassed. As years go by we're apt to see . . . . But that's it! . . . Enough with the golf! My new game will be Chinese checkers . . . easier to understand, y'know, and possibly only subject in the future to Federal Immigration and Naturalization scrutiny. We should be safe for awhile.

On average, 1950 through year 2000 was a marvelous adventure in sports. Let us pray to gain back some of our good sense and hope to do as well overall by the year 2050. Going forward, then, pattern your resolve on a time tested maxim: If you're not an athlete, be an athletic supporter. If you're not a team player, wear a cup!

Chapter Eleven

Political Bents

According to "Who's Who?", Columbus and his crew,
They landed here, that well-known year, of fourteen-ninety two.
Upon the shore to greet them, all the redmen were amassed;
They all wore funny make-ups, like a comic op'ra cast.
Columbus yelled, "What have we found? What can this island be?"
Said he, "Let's take a look around and see what we can see."
Indians and trees, Indians and trees;
That was all Columbus found, just a happy hunting ground.
Indians and trees, Indians and trees;
Seminoles and Cherokees; apple, peach and cherry trees.
Look what's happened, just look around today.
Look what's happened! It takes your breath away.
The greatest country on the earth, developed, if you please,
From fifty thousand Indians, and fifty million trees.[28]

"Indians and Trees" was just one of the songs my father parodied between 1938 and 1940. During his politicking days in Altoona, PA, in support of Republican candidates versus President Franklin

D. Roosevelt's Democratic machine, Dad and his friend, Jed Dickson, performed as a song and dance team in their own musical comedy skits and minstrel shows, usually at Shriners and Jesters' functions. They managed political parodies on such standards as "In The Shade of The Old Apple Tree" (Put The G.O.P Back in Its Place), "Oh! Susanna" (Oh! Thank Goodness, we've got them on the run), "Dinah," "I'll Never Say Never Again" and "Ragtime Cowboy Joe." Some of the lyrics were vigorously contrived. Others were clever. I never read or heard of any awards handed out for originality. But they prevailed as entertainers. In 1938 Dad and Jed successfully backed James Van Zandt—an Altoona railroader and coworker—for the United States Congress. In the 1940 presidential race, however, they bet the wrong horse. President Roosevelt took fifty-five percent of the vote from their man, Republican candidate, Wendell L. Willkie. The serious issues in those years—except for the threat of war in Europe—hardly registered on anyone's "critical scale." In fact, Willkie supported most things that Roosevelt was doing or proposing. The nation, facing the uncertainty of war in Europe, practically said, *Why change?* Even though it was to be FDR's third term (in four more years he would win another), people—except for Dad and Jed, that is—considered that life was relatively untroubled for the first time in years. True, the country was still in the throes of economic depression, but FDR—using the diversionary tactics of a carnival shill—since 1933 had stirred interest and hope in the masses with his "alphabetic" legislation and prime-the-pump fiscal policy. He concocted the CCC, the WPA, the TVA, and the NRA, to name a few. Many adored the man simply for repealing Prohibition in 1933. Up to then, drinking folks hadn't experienced a restful, legal snort since the old gray mare was a girl. But the nation, and the world, still remained a mess. World War II, sadly, arrived in the nick of time. We promptly forgot politics and economics and came together as a nation for the greater good.

Political rhetoric between opposing parties in those days lacked the divisiveness of today's so-called partisan politics of personal destruction. Politician's "zingers," as I remember, seemed almost sugar coated compared to the garbage dredged up these days—particularly from the Clinton years. Had the moral issues of the 1990s been alive back then, those involved would've been strongly censured, regardless of party affiliation. "Die-hards" will insist that Roosevelt, Eisenhower, and even Truman, had their secret peccadilloes. If so, the media was discreet and not so blind envious for a scoop. I rather think, however, that a stash of spare "babes," or even just one surreptitious intern skulking the White House innards after lights out, at any prior date in history—President Harding's tenure excluded—would've raised some pretty serious eyebrows. Bill and Hillary's Lincoln Bedroom capers, alone, would've shut the country down and sent the Arkansas hillbillies packing. Washington, DC, wasn't always about politics or some other cover-up. It *was* always about a semblance of integrity, or better.

Every citizen should be required to attend a class in Economics for Dummies and pass the course to be able to vote. Most just don't understand the difference between Democratic and Republican financial policy, and they need to know. The fiscal health of our country is critical. Intelligent voters elect responsible candidates. The Clinton Administration showed us that nothing was beneath them. They needed voter ignorance. They banked on it. Democrats in the year 2000 needed to stay in office to continue the cover-up for eight more years. Unwittingly, senior citizens and minorities were brow beaten into believing that Republicans were cheats and thugs, mainly on big ticket issues like social security and taxes. Every campaign has it's mud slinging. But *Der Lugnermeister* Clinton, throughout his tenure, had assembled a coalition of extremely competent liars. These guys could spin gold from maggot dung, and often were called to the task. Minorities—notably black Americans—have been getting the Democratic party line for forty years or more: *The vast conservative Republican conspiracy keeps you at the bottom of the economic ladder year after year. And—uh, by the way—while you're down there, you really do need the compassion and pabulum of the Democratic party for aid and sustenance.* The Clinton people were accused and proven guilty of many offenses. It was probably the tip of the iceberg. Never were they accused of "cooking" the government books. My guess is, however, that it was on their agenda. Starting in mid-2000, when Economic Indicators showed a decline in any category—regardless of degree—it seemed that Clinton's henchmen were right there to tell the country of another estimated five or ten trillion dollar surge in government surpluses. That farce continued until Clinton and crew left the scene. By then the surplus was astronomical and Clinton's poll numbers were through the roof. About six minutes after George Bush took the oath of office, CNN News was on the tube announcing that the bottom just fell out. According to the liberal TV and press, every company in existence was thinking "lay-off." The surplus was drying up like a prune on diuretics. Duh? When did this all happen? In the old days, absent the present "dumbed down" liberal base, Americans wouldn't have accepted that kind of "holier-than-thou" bullroar from the likes of Clinton and his sycophantic spin *meisters*. Even as kids, we'd have taken them up the nearest alley and beaten the crap out of 'em. In the past, in my own private way, I always personally approved of every United States President simply out of respect for our country and for the high office that he held. And that included Clinton, even after news of his "bedding a wench" went public. It was the dishonesty that did it for me. Curiously, I wonder, when did some of us learn to admire exposed corruption, immorality and depravity in our fellow man? Party lines are not the dividing lines here. Human decency is. And why did it take a national tragedy on September 11, 2001, to usher in a "new vision" to those same such individuals. Call it a senior moment, if you will; make no mistake, however, about my personal feelings. Politics aside, I am still appalled at the way otherwise normal and decent people treated President George (W.) Bush, even after knowing of Bill Clinton's proven sleazy record and background. Clinton's constant butchering of logic in defense of his actions was pathetic: " . . . I tried to walk a fine line between acting lawfully and testifying falsely. I now recognize that I did not fully accomplish this goal . . . ." He "knowingly violated" court rules and gave no answers that "were false," but "didn't knowingly give false answers."[29] It was reminiscent of another accomplished liar named Hoffa, i.e., " . . . to the best of my recollection, I must recall on my memory. I cannot remember."[30]

Paul Begala, of the Clinton *inner sanctum*, said Clinton deserves to be on Mt Rushmore. I say hoist'em both up—and high. How appropriate! Both have honed chiseling to an art form. There is this vignette from Begala, tutor of Al Gore for his year 2000 presidential debates with George Bush, as reported by Peggy Noonan in *The Wall Street Journal*: In reference to an electoral map of the United States, Begala indicated that states in red were for Bush, and those in blue belonged to Gore. However, he pointed out, a closer look at the red states showed a more complex picture: " 'You see the state where James Byrd was lynch-dragged behind a pickup truck until his body came apart—it's red. You see the state where Matthew Sheppard was crucified on a split-rail fence for the crime of being gay—it's red. You see the state where right-wing extremists blew up a federal office building and murdered scores of federal employees—it's red. The state where an Army private who was thought to be gay was bludgeoned to death with a baseball bat, and the state where neo-Nazi skinheads murdered two African-Americans because of their skin color, and the state where Bob Jones University spews its anti-Catholic bigotry: they're all red too.'

"It was a remarkably hate-filled column, but also a public service in that it revealed what animates Clinton-Gore thinking regarding their opponents: hatred pure and simple, a hatred that used to be hidden and now proudly walks forward."[31]

Another fine example of New Class journalism, on par with Begala's hate piece, comes from Maureen Dowd. Ms. Dowd, referring to something she dreamed up as "the Bush monopoly," writes: "Finally, Al Gore got wise. . . . He has stopped treating W. as a hapless daddy's boy and started treating him as the face of the ruthless Bush family cartel. . . . W. campaigned on the issue of restoring trust. But it turns out he meant restoring the Family Trust. The Bush monopoly, after all, has operated in the interregnum with the same arrogant philosophy as the Microsoft monopoly: You can have all the choice you want—as long as you choose us. . . ."[32] (A side note to the Microsoft fiasco: Bill Clinton promised to hunt down and punish at least six different terrorist acts during the 1990s. He did nothing. In reality he spent more time and money trying to *hunt down and punish* Bill Gates.)

As for the likes of Begala and Ms. Dowd, I ask: Where were you when Intellectual Curiosity 101 was last taught? Why can't you accept compassion, integrity and humanity as real, live, normal human traits, and not mere political buzz words? America needs your kind of daily stuff like Johnstown needs a flood. In 1954, Army Counsel Joseph Welch said to the arrogant, grandstanding Senator Joseph McCarthy (R-Wis) during McCarthy's brutal, uncaring hearings into possible communist activities in the U.S.Army: "Until this moment, Senator, I think I never really gauged your cruelty or recklessness. . . . Have you no sense of decency, sir, at long last? Have you left no sense of decency?" Later that year the Senate censured McCarthy and he faded from the national scene. Ditto that to Begala and Dowd.

I want a front row seat someday when we finally run the modern liberal sleaze bags from town. By their obvious parasitic nature and lack of personal integrity, I know the Clintons, Ted Kennedy and Begala will be among the last to be weaned from the public trough. It would be thrilling for their next step "over the line" to be the International Date Line. Senator Kennedy, with his background in nothing, couldn't meet the standards for "dog catcher" in most American towns. Yet, as a known "scofflaw," he sits on the powerful Senate Judicial Committee weighing judgement on appointees to the highest law positions in the land. Furthermore, he does it while accurately portraying the role of a deceitful, degenerate, old fool of a drunk. I am personally embarrassed to know that such ilk represent our country. Where does the Constitution say that we, as Americans, must tolerate scum to do the people's business? The rationale is, I suppose, that Mr. Kennedy has simply been occupying space in Congress for thirty some years and, therefore, is harmless. More's the pity.

Some media maniac once commented that Bill Clinton exhibits remarkable "grace under pressure." Most accomplished liars do. Given his trashy credentials, the comment could only refer to a known liaison somewhere—possibly with a lady named Grace—while *schtupping* her in Little Rock, AR, possibly at a place called The Shady Lady Trailer Park, during a fact finding tour on government boondoggles. Clinton would've later, no doubt, accused Republican opponents of dead-end tactics and no-win politics which he'd vow to avenge. The first new garbage scow built by our Navy should be christened USS William J. Clinton.

There was always something Carrollesque about Clinton when considering the tandem of Clinton and Reno in action—a pair to publicly "crucify" a Cuban child in exchange for "peace in our time" with Fidel Castro. Consider Carroll's "Mad Tea-party" from *Alice In Wonderland*:

"There was a table set out under a tree in front of the house, and the March Hare and the (Mad) Hatter were having tea at it. . . . The table was a large one . . . 'No room! No room!' they cried out when they saw Alice coming. . . .

'There's plenty of room!' said Alice indignantly. . . .

'Have some wine,' the March Hare said in an encouraging tone.

Alice looked all round the table, but there was nothing on it but tea. 'I don't see any wine,' she remarked.

'There isn't any,' said the March Hare.

'Then it wasn't very civil of you to offer it,' said Alice angrily.

'It wasn't very civil of you to sit down without being invited,' said the March Hare.

'I didn't know it was *your* table,' said Alice, 'it's laid for a great many more than three.'

Later Alice asks: 'Is that the reason so many tea-things are put out here?'. . .

'Yes, that's it,' said the Hatter with a sigh; 'it's always tea-time, and we've no time to wash the things between the whiles.'

'Then you keep moving round, I suppose?' said Alice.

'Exactly so,' said the Hatter, 'as things get used up.'

'But what happens when you come to the beginning again?' Alice ventured to ask. 'Suppose we change the subject,' the March Hare interrupted, yawning. 'I'm getting tired of this.' . . . ."[33]

In this version of the Carroll classic, Alice is played by a "mature" Elian Gonzales. The roles of the March Hare and Mad Hatter are played interchangeably by William Clinton—Arkansas' version of Willie "The Actor" Sutton, and Janet Reno—former "blocking" specialist from Florida football country.

Also, there was a U.S. Surgeon General somewhere during the Clinton years, thought suspect for recommending that school officials distribute flavored condoms to the boys so to prevent halitosis in the girls. That cost cutting proposal was delivered—no doubt, to

Her Generalship's desk from a "suggestion box" in a high school locker room somewhere—by a seventeen year old, public health advocate with more than just Georgia and "your run-of-the-mill orgasm" on his mind. And so it goes. . . . The small economies in office do make for a healthier, wealthier and wiser proletariat. It was a thankless job for Surgeon General Elders, but, somebody had to . . . etc., etc., etc. . . . *ad nauseam*. The bottom line: Clinton and cronies are political freaks. The fact of their lifetime "achievement" is an American disgrace.

So many Americans, it seems, don't think American anymore. We've become political items. We're strictly for or against. Where's the middle ground? Nothing's sacred to the modern political climate. Anti-heroes want the heroes vanquished. Ex-Senator Bob Kerry (D-Neb), former Navy Seal and medal of honor winner for bravery in Vietnam, is accused by a former Seal buddy of killing Viet women and children and accepting medals for it. As a continuing news expose', it's only the tip of the iceberg. Paul Harvey said it best: "In modern warfare there are no civilians." (4/26/01)

In my opinion, most of the media people today are in a feeding frenzy and totally out of hand. I'm convinced that during World War II, had the media—for nothing but top ratings—possessed the same political bias and killer instincts of today's news readers and writers, America would've lost the war, or still be fighting it. In the 1940s when FDR held a press conference and said that certain of his comments were off the record, they *were* off the record—no continuing dumb questions asked—or heads rolled.

Chris Matthews is a raw rookie compared to war correspondents before and after 1940. In his own league—reporting the political pratfalls of the Clintons and other reprobates—he's more than acceptable. On 9-11-01, as host of *Hard Ball*, he chose to expound on the New York Trade Center tragedy and the great "vanity" of Americans—Americans who don't seem to understand that many folks around the world just don't like them. Americans, he continued, don't realize that the days of winning global friendship with candy bars, as in W.W.II, is over. *Wall Street Journal* writer, Dorothy Rabinowitz, properly characterized Matthews' comments as "a round of blow hard pronouncements." In his regular column for the *San*

Francisco Chronicle Matthews continued in his vein of spastic, verbal diarrhea by expanding the W.W.II analogy. He compared the actions of President Bush in September, 2001, with those of Franklin D. Roosevelt in December, 1941. He implied in President Bush a lack of eloquence, knowledge, courage and leadership. As to Roosevelt, Matthews seemed to opine that FDR—like Moses in the wilderness—was practically able to appear with a slate of commandments (The War Powers Acts) to conquer Nazi Germany, Japan, and the Great Depression in the space of a single afternoon. Matthews needs to get a life with a proper viewpoint. For a fact, he, himself, hadn't been conceived into life until some years after 1941.

Around the time of Matthews' article, Maureen Dowd was getting her nasty two-cents worth in: ". . . Washington had the silence of the grave. . . . For much of the day we weren't sure where the president was. There were statements floating in from him from various secure zones in the air or underground. The vice-president was out of sight. And yet it was chilling to see how unprepared those in charge of planning seemed, after years of warning about just such an attack. . . . Even the president didn't seem sure of where to go. . . . And the White House is where he should be."[34]

In eloquence of speech and manner, George (.W) Bush isn't even close to FDR. But then, neither was Dwight Eisenhower. As to knowledge of the enemy, after weeks and months of the terrorism we still didn't know. FDR knew in a second to declare war against Germany and Japan. On the matter of courage, Matthews states: "FDR, despite his crippling polio, stood before Congress to declare war. . . . Bush headed to a bunker in Nebraska."[35] FDR actually stood before Congress the next day—12/8/41. And furthermore, FDR didn't have a bunker in Nebraska, or Poughkeepsie, or anywhere else. Nor did he have Air Force One or anything like it. It was a different time, a different war. George Bush acted according to the plan of war—his war. Finally, when it comes to leadership, time is the final judge. All great leaders were untested once. Great tragedies make great leaders. We should be thanking God—not slinging mud—for the presence of principled individuals in times of national crisis. We all have the potential for greatness. It is thrust only on a few. Give President Bush his just due. By all indications, he will find a worthy place in history. During World War II, the Office of War Information, through the press, radio and movies, made "psychological warfare" on the enemy. They proved that "media bombs" could be as deadly as the real item. All we can hope is that people like Matthews, Dowd and Peter Jennings, *et al*, use the influence and prestige of their powerful weapons to *unite* the cause, not confuse and divide America and the American homefront.

In addition to the home grown garden variety politician we must abide, there are even more dangerous hacks around the globe. These are the "world citizen types," the ones who engineered America's "booting" from the United Nations International Human Rights Commission, namely China and Cuba—a couple of real stand-up thugs. I say don't get mad. I say buy back the UN building and convert it into The New World Trade Center. Then China would be free to take a "slow boat to China" and Castro could take some fine Cuban cigars and shove'em where the sun will never shine. (Unless, hopefully, he should someday enjoy a similar "overexposure" as did Italian dictator Benito Mussolini in 1945. After being shot by former "loyal" subjects, Mussolini and his mistress were hung by the feet, butt-naked—as well as butt-dead—for display and a long needed tan in the streets of Milan.) The United States, it seems, sends billions in aid all over the world to anybody who asks. The world either wastes it or steals it. It's more politics as usual on a grander scale. America has always led the way in feeding the world. America doesn't want starvation anywhere. We even feed our enemies. While Bill and Hillary were traveling the planet, putting billions on the American tab, what else were they doing besides appeasing rogue nations? Did he ever ask other world leaders to "kick in a few bucks for the poor slobs in the next country." Or did he ever get really mad and say: "Do you guys have any responsibility in this world? . . . Do you know what America actually does for the world these days?" Do you think he ever looked those European monkeys square in the eye and said, "Remember when we bailed your sorry asses out of the muck after World War II?" We all know the answer is "no." Clinton and Arafat over the years were like a pair of painted turnstile puppets on a Swiss cuckoo clock: Arafat came over here for the mountain air; Clinton went over there for the "therapeutic waters." In foreign relations, I think, Clinton was the great appeaser—like Neville Chamberlain, only worse: Clinton had a wife as backer. Hillary's lies and half-truths gave "Tokyo" Rose rank amateur status. Here's a silly story. Fifty years ago *Mad Magazine* would've axed it for being too ridiculous. The emergence in the mid-1950s of the American Civil Liberties Union (ACLU) as a formidable force against violations to constitutional rights and other "jabberwocky"[36]—real or perceived—changed all that. These days, this story is practically what we are, dovetailing precisely with one or more of the political leanings that prospers inside our splendid democratic nation—a nation all the more splendid for allowing such tripe to openly flourish without the issuance of official edicts for public stoning, hanging, decapitation and/or castration.

With the rallying cry—"Imagine what the Journal could do for you."—a recent *Wall Street Journal* ad tells of two college graduates. Both begin their careers on an even field. One reads the Journal religiously. He attains great success. The other reads everything but the Journal and ends his days a contemptible failure. Both rise or fall because of *The Wall Street Journal*—no strings pulled, no peer or parental favors, no politics. No way!

More realistically the real story concerns the *left leaning* Toonerville, PA, *Daily Bugle* and two kindergarten boys on their first day at school. The first lad's mother—a professed conservative and talk radio newsaholic—vows the best for her son's budding years. Missing no opportunity to repel liberal tendencies, from the very start she decides on the *Daily Bugle* op-ed page as the wrapper of choice for her child's brown bag lunches. Since a normal dose of the Bugle's liberal tripe is always printed there, her undaunted charge is to see garbage-go-to-garbage. During the school's first scheduled meal period her son unwraps a chicken finger and, in a gesture to share, makes a pointing motion (as with hand gun) toward a skinny, poorly dressed, minority classmate. Their young teacher—a comely lass and past recipient of the NEA/Teamster "James R. Hoffa Humanitarian of the Year" award—instantly nabs the "chicken gun maniac" and hauls his tiny butt off to the office of Deputy Provost Marshal for Juvenile Affairs - Kindergarten Division, where the startled lad is fingerprinted, photo I.D.'d, deposed and suspended six weeks for violating the school's zero incidence policy. Displaying remarkable foresight, school authorities insert a permanent notation in the child's school record. Predictably, such a gaffe on his resume` prevents future scholarships, grants, loans, etc. Colleges refuse his applications. After high school he hops from job to job. Employers reviewing his "dubious" record typically regard him as a "last resort" hire. Eventually, falsely accused of embezzlement, for twenty-five years he rots away in a maximum security prison. His remaining days are endured exterminating dung beetles at a Brooklyn, New York museum.

The second child retrieves and eats the chicken finger that was offered. He becomes ill and throws up on the lunch wrapper—the *Daily Bugle* op-ed page. Fearing reprisals from school officials, the boy avoids detection by cleaning his mess with the newspaper and stuffing it inside an empty desk. The shriveled, crusty, stinking mass is discovered six weeks later by school authorities and traced back to the child. They call him forward for interviews. Suddenly he appears on the talk shows—Oprah and Rosie—where his fetid background of minority under-privilege is glorified and he is hailed profusely for his disciplined, free flowing, yet tenacious, artistic genius. Experts declare his project *an important work* and a masterpiece and title it *Vomitus in Adversaria*. The Carnegie Museum displays it. The National Endowment for the Arts awards him a scholarship for study in Paris. He is proclaimed a prodigy by all who know art. For a lifetime he is lauded as the foremost authority in the field of modern free form art composition, an honor that additionally cites the Toonerville, PA, *Daily Bugle* as a natural conduit for aptitude toward fame and attainment in the courtly arena of "World Success."

"Imagine what the Bugle could do for you!"

> "And all the monkeys aren't in the zoo,
> Ev'ry day you meet quite a few,
> So you see it's all up to you.
> You can be better than you are.
> You could be swinging on a star.[37]

Chapter Twelve

Anomalies

"I love to hear the rhythm of the clickety clack
And hear the lonesome whistle, see the smoke from the stack
And pal around with democratic fellows named 'Mac'
So, take me right back to the track, Jack!"[38]

    We get to pick our friends—democratic, or whatever. One of life's banes in maturity is the acquisition of *in-laws*. In-laws are thrust upon us with the wrath of God playing the devil. Over time, most of us survive . . . barely. Take my wife's family—please! (Pardon the self-indulgence. I swore not to use that chestnut.) The daily dose of negative thinking that flows from my sisters-in-law could've easily forced Norman Vincent Peale into a career move. As in-laws go, we can take 'em or leave 'em in fair times or foul; but 'till death or divorce, do us part, we'll always be joined at the hip.
    Another affliction of aging is our masochistic urge to trek from secure homes every five years so to confront former school chums

in a revelry of startling, mutual self-decay. It's the *class reunion*: anticipated by some, dreaded by some, and, as the years pass, ignored by more than a few. A goodly number of local alums actually are perpetual "no-shows." As invitations to class reunions go, I get more than my share these days, having attended two high schools as a senior, in addition to college some years later. I wasn't always in such demand by old chums, but as alumni get older reunion councils look harder, hoping to unearth from the dust a forgotten classmate, possibly one world famous, or simply a missing relic of the past, someone who had always cleverly escaped the "search and seizure" arm of the committee. Class reunion organizers, as years pile up, meet an ever more difficult struggle in presenting the past. The task they face is to re-create a status quo of the "good life" as we thought we lived it in 1951, or whatever graduation year we represent. That theory worked like a charm so long as we could all attend looking and acting like reasonably normal human beings. With each five year interval, however, the cracks began to show ever so slightly, then widened, and eventually broke apart. The 25th Reunion was the dividing line, I think. After that, each reunion presented a unique, defining moment for me, none of which ever furthered my resolve to keep coming back ". . . till the last dear companion drops smiling away . . ."[39] There was the 30th year affair when I recalled carelessly of a Friday night date in 1950, discovering too late that I was talking to her husband. At the 40th celebration a former girl friend showed up for the first time ever. She had hardly aged in forty years. I met her husband. She greeted my wife. They were uncomfortable together. I was uncomfortable. As it turned out, it was "hello" and "good-bye." She avoided me after that. Later, I overheard her husband ask, "What'd ya ever see in that guy?" Her answer said it all: "I used to like him." At a recent 50th reunion, I ran into another old beau. We'd dated for a year between 1951 and 1952. She was still an attractive and pleasant lady. During our dating years she had become too serious for my comfort level. Her ever increasing talk of marriage had scared the hell out of me. In 1952 I decided to "join the Navy and see Korea." At the reunion we had talked for about five minutes when she asked: "Who are you anyway?" With a decisive mental maneuver, I instantly bid "so-long, sayonara" to future festivities of a "re-unity" nature.

In the natural sequence of 50th reunions, I guess, my misery was not complete. Next to shatter the dream of eternal youth was an "out of the blue" appearance by some long, lost classmate who ages ago had been crowned something akin to: Most Likely to be the Next Miss America From the Class of '51. She managed this "coming out" after fifty years, I'm sure, by resurrecting every available corpuscle in her struggling body. She barely achieved a pale resemblance to Whistler's mother's mother. Still fashion conscious, she was sporting black, high top, orthopedic shoes, stylish—no doubt—at the turn of the century when first worn by schoolmarm Annie Taylor as she went over Niagara Falls in a barrel. Surreptitious whispers circulated as every classmate in the room struggled to learn her identity. Once the secret was out, just as surreptitiously, a few guests at a time began ambling to the one or two yearbooks lying about the place for a curious peek at this long lost "world beauty," circa 1951. For me, her return from the dusky netherworld held one more depressing surprise as I recalled that I had been the chosen escort of this "Miss Whatsername" at *that* dubious award ceremony years ago. It all came back to me. People had called us a "cute couple" afterward. But, . . . *it's not possible to look that old!!!* I screamed silently to my inner self. I distinctly remember . . . well, er . . . sort'a remember . . . that Mrs. Walters held her back about fifteen years in freshmen Latin. That consoled me for about half-a-minute 'til I accepted that my inner self was telling me an out-and-out lie. . . . Regardless, if we both were so cute in 1951 . . . what recent avalanche was she just found under? . . . Was it a major epidemic she barely survived? . . . And more frightening: *Who the hell am I to talk? . . . I must look like the only Titanic survivor hit by the iceberg!* At least one thing became crystal clear. I knew the reason for classmate's odd stares, and rushing to do other things as I approached them during the festivities.

On the brighter side: At these later reunions, I met many "young" lady alumnae who, fifty years earlier, had been as plain and exciting as gray paint; ladies who now oozed personality and charm like the guy who first taught Dale Carnegie "how to win friends and influence people." At its best, the reunion scene, as I kept advising myself, was a real "pair-a-ducks," an oxymoron. So, following my own advice for times of trouble and stress, I adopted a fall-back position: *Lie low at the bar for a spell!*

Life threatening scenes similar to that of the "Miss Whatsername" caper I'm sure are constantly played out during the events of any class reunion. And to think it'll only get worse if we let it. One of my theories is that sometime around the 25th year anniversary the more inventive alums start hiring young actors to show up as stand-in classmates. It's a way to stay on the mailing list and still get a class picture every five years without exposing one's true, withering identity to collegial curiosity. As the years pass, the vanity and dilemma of age hints at crisis proportions for a few—not for yours truly, of course. I carry a perpetual mental picture of myself that flies straight from the senior yearbook to the last dance and last farewell and, finally, to the last car of the last alum leaving town from the last reunion, at the end of the last reunion week-end

Another *life* experience, usually from the class "get re-acquainted" session, is about running into the phony intellectual type. Here's this guy you don't even recognize. He's got a stinking, Harvard yard, thing for a pipe clenched in his teeth. Under one arm he's pressing a petite volume of *The Rubaiyat* as he waves the other arm and calls your name at the peak of a screeching voice. Funny. These kinds always remember me. Usually it had to do with once sitting together in detention class, or being nailed on a "playing hookey" charge. It was never for anything connected with high honors or anything worthwhile. It was always the rotten stuff. Now he's back in my face after fifty years to remind me that I'm still a bum and he, on the contrary, has just won the Nobel prize for literature. This particular guy I'm remembering was once the class dunce, would you believe. He began by regaling me with tales of his home library: "I'm reading at least a dozen books constantly. . . . Nothing but 'the classics,' you know. I keep Tolstoy in my bathroom reading rack." He paused. I said, "It must be a big rack." He paused again and thought, then snorted and let out a roar. Finally realizing that I'd said something very stupid or very clever, he added: "Whatever that means," and slipped away in search of less nitpicking pedants. I've noticed this, too, about alumni personalities: The older they get the closer they grow toward family and tend either to forget or downplay old friends at reunions—or not show up at all.

In our dotage I believe we keep alive some indelible image of ourselves, an impression of what we had been, or wanted to be. Possibly there's a reflection there of some dashing young *twentyish* lad or lass, in body and spirit invincible before the world, in quest of life's answer to eternal youth. Is it that, rather than the certain knowledge that self and once splendid school friends, each in a specific time and fashion, must accept the destiny of "how we got this way" and pass on to a higher plain? Whether in fact or fiction we actually once had been *dashing* is moot; when we think young, we are young. It works most of the time. As I grow older, maintaining the youthful perception becomes difficult. I follow three helpful rules. I avoid: camera close-ups; group photos, unless in the very back row; and mirrors, except when hidden behind shaving cream or brushing my teeth wearing extra dark sunglasses.

Mentally, class reunions have become an exercise in pent-up futility, humiliation and hostility. Over the years, some close friends have turned into social anomalies. It's a fact of aging, I suppose. I admit to being at least fifty percent of the problem. We are what we are. People and times change. Extended absence, naturally, makes evolution seem more acute and noticeable. My high school best friend and his wife had been neighbors as well as friends. She had always been skittish about potential, personal health problems. Over a period of ten reunions, skittish had blossomed to full-fledged hypochondria. To stretch the point, the word "humorous" uttered within her earshot might have triggered severe, imagined upper arm pain. Talk about self-centered and illusory aches and illness, or about a superiority complex and "control freak" syndrome; talk about a pain in the ass! She'd imagined more pain and suffering over fifty years than Sister Theresa ever confronted on four continents. During this same time frame her husband and his personality went to hell in a handcart. They were made for each other. (How do we age gracefully?) At each reunion when we met, I sensed the extremes in his disposition drifting respectively toward the worst of Al Capone and Pee Wee Herman. As husband and wife they'd become music haters—and let you know it. She hated sports—and let you know it. She couldn't have forced a smile at Mach 2. Oddly, a trace of humor occasionally peeked out from his supercilious exterior. His habit in public was a great show of largesse (not Italian for *fat rear end,* but in this case it fit). At restaurants he lunged for the check as adroitly as boardwalk sea gulls troll for popcorn scraps, generally throwing his money and influence around, only to look for collection in private, later. He *never* accepted a "treat," or a "buy ya a beer" offer in a public place. Her knack of steering conversations toward her "delicate condition" was as slick as an ice patch awash in quicksilver. With age, he began suggesting an expertise as a self-taught chef and food service master. Simultaneously, at meals he had become finicky—the sight of rare meat practically rendered him convulsive. Was this the same guy who had survived four years of U.S. Army chow? Once during a reunion week-end, while driving in congested traffic in a heavily ethnic neighborhood in the middle of downtown Harrisburg, Pennsylvania—his hometown—he panicked. This from a man with a background as a military policeman. We continued to click in other areas of interest. But I had changed, too. After retirement I chose to wean myself from former friends not avid in music and/or sports. Music shows good humor and joy of spirit; athletics displays an affinity for competition and teamwork—qualities essential to ward away both *post-reunion* and *pre-retirement* depression.

 A final comment on class reunions concerns a lost link to our former teachers and professors, often ordinary women and men who only gained our respect long after being dead and buried. High school or college graduation draws a defining line between "prehistoric" school days and the "pop culture" of subsequent life. Abandoned to the back burner of memory is this coterie of *ancients* who once shaped our lives and futures as surely as parents. Typically they remain *personae non gratae* until our 25th reunion comes 'round when, abruptly, we understand the fact of our own mortality. Their faces appear in our thoughts, as their names pepper ordinary conversation. Sadly, by then most are gone. Some we knew by proper names we'd never forget: Coach James, Mrs. Gardner; others we recalled from a nickname: Zeke, Stoney, Buggy. Others we remembered from some outstanding or quirky, personal characteristic. But, oh, to have them back in the flesh, to share even one reunion evening on talk of specific things on a level field.

The late, Miss Jeanette Wentz, and her, also late, sisters were four extremely fine ladies. We were all neighbors once, atop Brewery Hill in Tylertown, PA. All the sisters were spinsters or widows and moderately up in years in the early 1940s during my elementary school years. Their collective worlds consisted of church and Sunday School, old-maidish attire and tons of hair piled high with a bun-in-the-back. Jeanette was the exception. She taught third grade at Tyler Elementary School and was my teacher there when I was eight years old. During her career she had taught my mother and father and aunts and uncles and untold cousins and friends. Miss Wentz was a *saint* who, five days a week, turned teaching into a "contact sport." Her methods were stern, sometimes physical, done, I'm sure, from a dedicated, inner compassion intended to instill her personal seal of excellence into each third grader fortunate enough to receive the least shred of knowledge she ever knew to impart. On her agenda, no child was lost or left behind. She saw to it. Looking back, my first impression is to know that "she scared the hell out of me." Her toughness, I think, by comparison, could've made Vince Lombardi and his Green Bay Packers look like Tiny Tim "tip-toeing through the tulips." Through all of her teaching years I'm sure she got the job done everytime.

In the America of today, Miss Wentz's principles and teaching methods would've put her behind bars for life. Guaranteed, by Christmas break of her first year teaching, some zealous ACLU "genius" would've prosecuted her off to the tightest maximum security "slammer" in the state, thus saving countless third graders—present and into the future—from the insidious effects of the callous education indifference of a capitalistic society. Consider her "rap" sheet: She'd have racked up violations against civil rights, human rights, social rights, the Bill of Rights, non-observance of labor unions strike rights, inciting to riot, non-observance of church/state separation laws, and, probably, failure to strip-search students in compliance with classroom "zero tolerance" reporting rules. It's the plain truth that an obviously "flawed" teacher, the ilk of Nettie Wentz, would've promptly been drummed from the system. Cries would've gone out to: "Bring back the firing squad," so they could shoot her, instead, during morning recess. My guess is that "Nettie" Wentz never gained *any* student's genuine respect until at least thirty-five years after third grade had passed. How regrettable!.

Rarely do I go ballistic on a subject of today versus yesterday . . . except in matters of *work ethic*s. An old proverb states, in effect, not to judge or criticize another until you have walked a mile in his shoes. Certain individuals living today couldn't even finish the trip without two cigarette breaks and a half-hour off for lunch. For awhile there's been a serious discrimination problem within our modern labor movement, specifically: between the workers versus non-workers. It applies to union and non-union labor alike. One expects such "slacking off" in the union shop, where, for decades, "big labor" has acted deliberately to undercut company profits via diluted efficiencies and unreasonable benefit demands. And do you believe it? Nowadays there's even a teacher's union—is it part of the Teamsters yet? Before ever approving of that craziness, a few of my old teachers—Nettie Wentz and Zeke Lepore, perhaps—would've had to be running it. With their kind of leadership we'd, at least, know the whereabouts of Jimmy Hoffa today. He'd either be clapping Nettie's dirty erasers in the back school yard, or be with Zeke on the football practice field doing "head-on tackle" drills. Although I could write a book and title it: "My Four Years of Involuntary Servitude Inside 'The Brotherhood of Electrical Workers Union'," I won't. I refer here, instead, to the railroad and steel industries where we still feel the economic effects of earlier year's questionable union practices. "Featherbedding" in labor relations is slang for union rules that limit productivity, allegedly to provide easy jobs or to prevent unemployment.[40] In the early 1960s the nation's railroads completed a project that replaced all steam locomotives with diesel engines. The diesel engine, among other things, eliminated the need for the fireman position aboard locomotives system wide. A strong railroad union used *featherbedding* and forced the railroads to employ firemen on diesel locomotives. It was a maneuver that contributed to continuing high labor costs and erosion of competitive edge in the railroad industry's peaking troubles against the burgeoning airline industry for passenger and freight revenues. The railroad transportation industry struggled mightily for survival through the 1960s. Railroads accounted for almost 70 percent of total passenger-miles by public carrier in 1930. By 1970 they accounted for less than one percent. In 1971 the National Railroad Passenger Corporation, a federal agency—known as Amtrak—was formed to take over the country's ailing railroad passenger service. Today air carriers dominate public intercity passenger transportation in the United States.

In the early 1960s, the militant unionism of the United Steelworkers forced the steel industry to accept a benefit package that included the "thirteen week" vacation for qualified hourly employees. Eligibility for this "bonanza" occurred every five years. Various other liberal benefits accrued during the in-between-years. The "thirteen week" package was a disaster. Following its implementation, the mill towns in and around Pittsburgh, PA experienced a brief economic boom—particularly in the bars of Homestead, Duquesne, McKees Rocks and Clairton—as vacationing steelworkers with time and money to spend "hung out." The good times, however, were short lived. Too much vacation was left at the end of the money. Steelworker domestic relations got a blackeye as marital difficulties surfaced, with divorce and separation rates increasing in most steel towns. Corporate profits suffered from these ultra-liberal union payouts. In order to avoid a disgruntled management, United States Steel Corporation, for one, made matching payments to all non-union employees in an equivalent amount to the expanded union vacation benefits. The only stipulation was that non-union employees received the benefit as cash deposits into individual Management Savings Accounts. Subsequently, economic stagnation and recession plagued the steel industry. Intensified foreign competition brought about permanent lay-offs and, naturally, loss of union membership. Legislation brought extensive government control over both labor and management in the form of: the Equal Pay Act, Equal Employment Opportunity Act, ERISA (pension reform), and OSHA (safety and health). Most major steel producing towns, especially around Pittsburgh, ultimately closed as parent companies diversified. It's no surprise, therefore, that labor unions these days are concerned more with job security than higher pay and benefits.

Non-union shops, as well, have their share of "renegade management," with trouble spots centered mainly throughout smaller service and manufacturing establishments. Many have righted themselves to successfully resist big labor organization. Others out there are ripe for the picking, with "goon mentality" managers abusing employee rights at every chance for a bigger bottom line. Don't misunderstand, profit is good as long as the cost excludes unfair pay and unfair practices dictated from the top. As everyone knows, labor unions exist largely due to management's failure back in the early years of the twentieth century. Established compensation programs didn't exist, then. There were no wage and hour laws. The standard work week consisted of "as long as it takes" to get the job done. Concepts such as incentive plans, benefit plans, minimum wage laws, child labor laws and standard working conditions were deliberately ignored by management. There are isolated "sweat shops" around today in America where similar conditions still exist. It seems to me that the ideal work place endures in the organization where each worker toils efficiently for a piece of the profits; where no employee is counter-productive due to union protection, because there is no union; and where inefficiency and quality is constantly monitored through proper controls and employee accountability. In other words: organizational excellence is the product of enlightened management and a skilled, goal oriented staff—devoid of union influence and latent inefficiency.

The "complaint" window of yesteryear has turned into the Customer Service Department of today. The term "customer service" is a relatively modern term in commerce; the "service" part of it, however, is often a long gone thing of the past. Some Customer Service Departments are as big as the Sales Departments they support. I remember shopping for a car several years ago. My wife and I had just taken a new Chrysler van for a test drive. I was ready to close the deal. Unfortunately, my salesman had other thoughts. It had just turned five p.m. on a Saturday afternoon—closing time at the dealership. The salesman said he'd return Monday: "Lock it up when you're done. Have a nice week-end." I bought a car the following Monday, from a different salesman, at another dealer. Also, too many times I have eaten at restaurants where the waitress has her eye on a 20 percent tip before she proceeds to give out her normal rotten service.

My favorite service provider has become the trash collector. These guys should be wearing surgical gloves and a mask. Over my trash cans each week, they perform like denim-clad brain surgeons. Separate containers are required for everything these days. They could use the Periodic Table of Elements as a handy reference guide. There's a bin for glass, plastic, metal, construction debris, paper and, finally, just plain old garbage. Before touching a thing, however, they survey the entire offering for "valuables," daintily removing this or that item, or piece of junk, with a stick, as if attending an archeological dig at King Tut's tomb. Anything worth salvaging is frantically stashed in some "secret place" deep within the bowels of their trash hauler. It's heartening to know that the Hope Diamond will be secure should it ever be plucked from my garbage. Finally, my pile of debris needs to be precisely sorted according, no doubt, to some rigid, pre-set standard established by our regional GAGAT (generally accepted garbage and trash) principals Board of Governors. If not up to snuff, the driver —*l'homme de garbage*—has the final word. A thumbs-down decision means the whole stinking mess stays put at the curb—except for the impounded *valuables,* of course—which, as in maritime law, have instantly become rightful property of one or more of my trash persons. While I'm left to deal with five tons of "de-certified" garbage at the curb, I'm comforted knowing that my former *family jewels* have passed on to discriminating collectors. They'll be safe, I know, inside that garbage truck "vault" and by day's end, PDQ, be under the appraiser's eye.

During World War II, particularly in the Pacific Theater, how did the Navy Seabee's manage to build roads and airfields in a matter of days? Modern highway crews need months . . .sometimes years. There are three stages to the modern work day cycle:

• Before clocking in - Complaint: I'm too sick to work today.
• During work - Complaint: It's not my job.
• After clocking out - Complaint: Man! I worked my butt off. Time for some R&R.

Featherbedding re-visited: Could it be a coincidence? Recently I cancelled my Sears credit card. The next day's business news reported 4,900 Sears office employees terminated nationwide. Was it overstaffing, or simply zealous attention to my customer needs?

As a youngster in 1944/1945, I delivered, via foot power, the Baltimore Sun to about one hundred neighborhood customers every evening after school, and on Saturday afternoons. My papers were delivered *per customer specs*: onto the porch, inside the mailbox, or precisely at the front door. As for my own paperboy, today, I never see or hear from him—except for a card at Christmas requesting: "Give generously. I'll be going to Harvard soon." His deliveries come out of the passenger-side window of a parent/chauffeur-driven, Lincoln town car. The paper isn't exactly "launched" toward the house. The lad barely delivers it. Generally, it gets to the curb where it lies about fifty feet from my door. On winter days it seems more like five hundred. . . . Did I mention? I also delivered The Grit when I was ten.

As part of President Franklin D. Roosevelt's New Deal program to fight the ravages of the Great Depression in 1933, several programs were established to reduce the effects of a 25 percent unemployment level which hung over America. Thus was born the Civilian Conservation Corps and the Public Works Administration. These were the first agencies to employ many people while helping to improve the nation's infrastructure. The Tennessee Valley Authority (TVA) was also formed and is still in existence today as the nation's largest utility firm. The TVA harnessed the power of the Tennessee River for the first time and helped lift that region out of dire poverty. A second phase of the New Deal was launched in 1935 with the passage of the Social Security Act and the Works Progress Administration (WPA)—later changed to Works Projects Administration. The WPA employed 8 million Americans between 1935 and 1942 to build roads, schools, airports, and other public works. As a kid in the early 1940s, I remember WPA gangs working around our Brewery Hill neighborhood, mostly paving or re-paving the roads. Of the 8 million in the program, it seemed that 7 million were on our block. We kids found joy as their antagonists. Variously, we threw stones and called them members of the "We Poke Along" club, or part of the "Women's Panties Association" (pretty racy stuff for little kids in those days). None of them, as I recall today, showed "road runner" enthusiasm, or a "be happy in your work" expression. But the projects got done. Many still stand today. As Americans, we supported their honest efforts. The country was too poor for welfare then, which meant no welfare or unemployment check for which to lie around and wait. Unknown then to us all, many would soon be gone to war, and many after that, simply, tragically gone. They weren't such bad guys, after all. "Every calling is great when greatly pursued."[41]

As anomalies go, race is a risky subject. It's so easy to express sincere personal feeling at the end of the day, then suddenly be declared a racist in the morning. Therefore, about race, I have little to say, except: Hooray! I finally made it. I'm a minority. I'm a white, Protestant male, pushing seventy. Is it a good thing or bad? AARP says to join their club and I'll be a "special interest group," too.

Years ago when I attended school in Tylertown, classes consisted of whites and blacks and one or two Orientals. People then lived and worked where they wanted to live and work. I was never aware of racial problems or tensions. Perhaps, I was too young. I believe that no one else was aware, either. I believe that the whites and blacks and Orientals became aware only after leaving Tylertown. At least, it's the truth with me.

Through all the passing years, two thoughts (or images) are foremost in my mind about race relations in America: Why was the multi-talented Nat King Cole allowed to be "booed" and dragged in humiliation off of a stage in 1956 in Birmingham, Alabama? And why do some blacks degrade other blacks who have obviously made it? Is it racial, political or social?

The dream of every senior in retirement—after unabated, consensual sex—should be travel. At least you would think it—travel by bus, no less. I, for one, hate busses and bus trips. Two seconds into a bus and I need the bathroom. To read the travel ads, you'd think "travel by bus" was the only thing seniors could do without a keeper. On the other hand, if you just happen to belong to the Moose, the Elks and a couple Happy Hours Clubs you can stay inside a bus for the rest of your days. You could make The Wandering Jew seem like a small town, flagpole sitter. Flying is worse. The only way a non-flyer should fly is with a double scotch in each hand and a stewardess on the way down the aisle with two more. Try walking. You'll love it. It's the old fashioned way.

Suddenly we have role models again. To our everlasting sorrow it took the devastation of an inhuman tragedy to bring it about. Like the old days we're openly praising firemen and policemen once more. The American flag is back in vogue. Patriotic fervor is practically at the heart of all we do. Will the aura persist? It's to see.

In these times, individuals from yesteryear come to mind, folks I can barely think of without getting teary-eyed. So many of these men and women came out of the second world war era, a time in history hardly close to imagination prior to today's crisis of terrorism. "Life, liberty and the pursuit of happiness . . ." was chock full of pure patriotism, loyalty to person and cause, and belief in a higher power. Hopefully, it's back to stay.

The anomaly of "awards" is subtle. Often movie stars get awards in recognition of an on-screen and off-screen ability to speak the f-word the most times without taking a breath or stuttering. Where is Ethel Barrymore when we need her most? Men and women who receive awards for "best this" or "best that" or "best whatever," are often described as "no nonsense" types. There are exceptions, of course, but it's a phony trait, indicative of individuals lacking humanity and without a sense of "native humor." To a point, I believe in "not suffering fools," but the so-called *no nonsense* person is usually rude and crude, an individual who considers impatience to be one of life's greatest virtues. Life is too short to spend a career in turmoil. Lend a hand along the way. Treat people as you want to be treated. Get mad when they start acting like *assholes*.

Bill Clinton, the First Role Model, accomplished a gigantic disservice to the youth of America. He reacted strictly from poll data. Unfortunately, no data was ever gathered from young folks, no poll taker was ever interested in young opinions. Clinton and his followers are, and were, weak in the principles that made America great. That lack of resolve weakened this great country as certainly as the surefire accuracy of women's intuition strengthened it. Possibly, liberals were taken over by a "pod invasion" from outer space sometime after 1992. I guess it's okay to forgive them, but for many folks it's difficult to forget. It would be truly miraculous to see all of our leaders and legislators shed their political "cocoons" and step forward as statesmen.

I won't say I don't know or admire any, maybe I do, but I hate to hear hyphenated American nationalities and family names.

The day I retired was the day I started full-time to wear dungarees and a baseball hat. From the beginning I wore the hat correctly—with the front in the front and the back in the back. That way, if anyone was silly enough to emulate me as a role model, my hat would be worn straight. If I had returned from a forty year coma and looked at today's teen-age fashion icons, with the shoes and the pants, I would swear that Yogi Berra was our national hero. Except, when Yogi wore his hat backwards he also wore a mask, chest protector, knee and shin protectors along with it. In retrospect, he cut a role model's dashing swath for his many admirers of the 1950's and 1960's. If you really want to emulate Yogi Berra: Start wearing a catcher's mask and play ball. They no longer call them the "tools of ignorance." He was, and is, a classy guy.

Barbara Bush gets my vote for the classiest lady around today from the old days. In our modern social cliques, a lady seems aptly defined "classy" upon her own recital of the modest *tattoo* sculpted to either of her unmentionable ass cheeks.

One more anomaly remains. I recently heard of a lemon scented, closet air freshener on the market with an ingredient that causes cancer in California. I'm relieved and grateful for the warning. I will stay out of California closets.

Chapter Thirteen

Look To the Future

"... the future is only the past again, entered through another gate."⁴²

"I asked my paw where did they go, when folks went courtin' years ago;
With no amusements like we have today.
The radio was then unknown, they just had grandma's gram-a-phone,
But still they fell in love and life was gay.

They didn't have no airy-planes, didn't have no streamlined trains,
But they had lonely country lanes, WHEN PAW WAS COURTIN' MAW.
They didn't have no ritzy bars, fancy drinks and caviars,
But they had lots of moon and stars, WHEN PAW WAS

COURTIN' MAW.

They didn't have no commentator with the news broadcast.
They listened on the 'party line' and got the news darn near as fast.
They didn't have electric light, just by lamps they'd spoon each night,
But still and all they did alright, WHEN PAW WAS COURTIN' MAW."[43]

If *past* precedes prologue and prologue isn't *present*, then prologue is *future*. Solving for X (past) makes *past equals future*. Ergo! Nowadays is the time they talked of back then. The future's upon us again. *"What a revoltin' development this is!"*[44]

I recoil at the fact of people today who, while *in sync* to volatile world conditions, remain *in denial* and scoff at thoughts of Americans having to give up certain freedoms simply because a gang of "two-bit" terrorists started blowing up the world. Those folks should wonder about, and relive, the "future" of some sixty years ago when American citizens—from barely aware babes-in-arms to mind-fading dowagers and graybeards—learned the hard lesson of World War Two: the lesson that freedom equals rights. And while some rights get trampled in the battle, they come back when we've won the war and, thus, freedom returns. Freedom is to fight for—not once and done—but always. Painful evidence emerged during the War years that the world had been, was and probably always would be chock-full of nuts: "mad scientist" types and terrorists, as well as other major and miscellaneous vermin.

On Sunday afternoon, December 7th, 1941, I was an eight year old child living in central Pennsylvania. My mother had ordered me to, "Quick! Run to the Sutton's. See if those Japs are headed this way." The Sutton sisters were our cousins and lived across the street from us on Brewery Hill in Tylertown, PA. Their brother, Bob, was with the U.S.Army in the Pacific. That fact, and the non-existence of substantive radio news about the Japanese sneak attack on Pearl Harbor, gave Mother, I'm sure, a distorted sense of geography, as well as a feeling that the Sutton's were "direct connected" to cousin Bob in the Fiji Islands. Everyone was terrified that afternoon. From a youngster's perspective, seeing visibly scared adults made for one petrified little boy.

Sunday, December 7th, was an unseasonably warm, sunny day. In New England pussy willows had suddenly sprouted. In New York City stores were packed with Christmas shoppers. It was the final day of the professional football season as 27,000 spectators sat in Washington, D.C.'s Griffith Stadium to watch quarterback Sammy Baugh lead the hometown Redskins to a 20-14 victory over the Philadelphia Eagles. During the game—as many fans later noted—the public-address system seemed to be paging an inordinate number of military VIP's for urgent phone calls. The aura of days had been getting cheerier then—particularly that December. Christmas was near and throughout the country people finally were getting back to work again as we slowly arose from the depths of the Great Depression. Americans had new found money to spend. Movie houses were packed to watch Greta Garbo in *Two-Faced Woman*. Oddly, the latest hit song of the day was "I Don't Want to Set the World on Fire" by The Ink Spots. Although parts of Europe and Asia had been fighting for several years, war was never an option for America. In addition to a staunch isolationist movement across the land, President Franklin D. Roosevelt had constantly promised American parents that their sons would never fight in any foreign war.

Bombs were still falling in Hawaii when the unbelievable news reached most Americans by radio. Millions were tuned to CBS that afternoon just as the New York Philharmonic was about to start Shostakovich's Symphony No. 1. The familiar voice of John Daly broke in shortly after 3 p.m.: "We interrupt this program to bring you a special news bulletin. The Japanese have attacked Pearl Harbor." Most folks asked: "Where? . . . *Pearl Harbor*?" They hadn't a clue. They did suspect, however, that a catastrophe had happened and that America was in trouble. At that same moment, isolationist Senator Gerald Nye of South Dakota was speaking at a Pittsburgh, PA, *America First* rally, telling a crowd of enthusiasts why the country should avoid all foreign wars. When a reporter handed him a note about Pearl Harbor, Nye remarked: "It sounds terribly fishy to me." Pearl Harbor was the worst homefront, war-related disaster in U. S. history prior to September 11, 2001. It had been the most galvanizing event ever in the lives of millions of Americans.

The fact of Pearl Harbor ignited our worst fears throughout the entire American population. Coastal defenses were immediately under way on all shores in anticipation of German and Japanese invasions. Landlocked border states worried about attacks through Canada or Mexico. In Wisconsin there was an appeal by the American Legion headquarters to create a guerrilla force composed of the state's 25,000 licensed deer hunters—". . . a formidable foe for any attackers," they insisted. In San Francisco, a jittery sentry on the Bay Bridge shot and wounded several motorists who were slow to stop at a checkpoint. Anti-aircraft batteries in Los Angeles fired at imaginary warplanes, with shell fragments falling from the sky, injuring dozens of scared residents below. Every city and town in America immediately established air raid procedures. At first there were numerous alarms—all false—that created major panic all around. Across the nation warnings by top military personnel and city officials were dire. Gun emplacements showed up instantly on rooftops in major cities and shore points. Searchlights scoured the night sky looking for enemy warplanes. Nervous citizen groups called for construction of bomb shelters. Others sought the refuge of caves and mine shafts. Blackout curtains—black cloth—were tacked up in homes and apartments, while civilian wardens patrolled most neighborhoods during air-raid drills.

The early months of 1942 were the darkest days of the War. Initial enthusiasm had faded and, although juke boxes around the country blared with tunes such as "Good-bye, Mama, I'm Off to Yokohama" and "You're a Sap, Mister Jap," British forces in the Pacific were being wiped out. Guam fell, then Singapore, Bataan and Corregidor. At home, the German U-boat fleet had become the scourge of the Atlantic Ocean—from Canada to the Caribbean and Gulf of Mexico. From January through May of 1942, eighty-seven ships were sunk in American waters.

Before the moment of Japan's sneak attack there were about 900,000 aliens of German, Italian and Japanese birth living in America. Our government was particularly concerned by the German population, since the German-American Bund, a Nazi front group, had been staging boisterous rallies in the German sections of certain cities, notably New York City and St. Louis. Italian-Americans were not considered a threat since, as President Roosevelt said of them, ". . . they are a lot of opera singers, . . ." There was serious talk among many—as some have now done since 9-11-01—concerning the loss of one's hard earned freedoms. In February, 1942, a few months after war was declared against Japan, approximately 112,000 American born citizens of Japanese descent were rounded up from their homes—mostly on the west coast—and exiled to "camps" in six western states and Arkansas. Through the auspices of the 1942 War Relocation Authority, our government, ostensibly to protect Japanese-Americans from the focus of hatred and resentment being carried out by mainstream American vandals and vigilantes, was instrumental in the formulation of this singular dark period for race relations in America's history. Significantly, not a single Japanese-American was ever brought to trial for espionage. In truth, during the immediate months after Pearl Harbor, few Americans even had the good sense to think, or power to act, calmly as it concerned the well-being of American born citizens of alien extraction. Sadly, a standard declaration surfaced in reference to the Japanese: "A Jap's a Jap!"

After Pearl Harbor, all recruiting stations were mobbed by volunteers. Everybody wanted into the act. World War One, General of the Army, John J. "Black Jack" Pershing, aged 81 and infirm, was driven to the White House from his suite at the Walter Reed Medical Center to offer his services. Film star Jimmy Stewart worked to fatten his "skin and bones" so as to meet the minimum weight standards for the Army Air Force. University of Chicago economics professor Paul Douglas, aged 50, joined the Marines as a buck private. Anyone of military age and not in uniform, unless physically or mentally impaired, was immediately suspect as to having "influential friends in high places" or, a congenital dose of a lack of courage. During World War Two, there were notably few attempts at draft dodging. (Compare that to subsequent conflicts and wars.) Late in the War, at any given time, there were 12 million individuals in the service—one of every 11 Americans served. At home, healthy men in civvies became a rarity. In professional baseball, the St. Louis Browns even used a one-armed outfielder named Pete Gray in their starting line-up. A popular song in 1943 lamented the lack of available civilian males: "They're either too young or too old; . . . they're either too bald or too bold."[45]

In the early days before American war production caught up with the recruiting rush, military training was frequently performed with make-believe guns and tanks. Machine guns were carved from two-by-fours. Placards, hung on Ford trucks, designated them as tanks. Equipment was in short supply. In the Louisiana maneuvers of summer, 1941, Major General George S. Patton, Jr. commanded an ill-equipped armored division. Patton's tanks were so old that they constantly broke down. A mechanic told him that the Army couldn't get certain spare parts, but they were available from the Sears and Roebuck mail order department. Patton immediately sent off a mail order for the needed parts and got his tanks back up and running, paying Sears later from his own pocket.

Early in the War, enlistment opened up for women. There was an immediate rush to serve. Women in uniform, however, were viewed as second-class citizen-soldiers. They endured the derision of their fellow GIs as well as that of civilians. They were alternately accused of lesbianism and heterosexual promiscuity. There was much fear that they would get PWOP—"pregnant without permission." A Marine officer was cruder. "Goddam it all," he told his first female arrivals. "First they send us dogs. Now it's women."

Prejudice encountered by women was mild compared to that encountered by blacks. The 961,000 blacks in the service faced a caste system far more inflexible than the discrimination they knew as mere civilians. During most of the War, strict racial segregation prevailed. Blacks had separate eating and recreational facilities. A black officer could not out-rank a white officer. In the beginning, the Navy accepted blacks only as mess attendants. The Marines would not accept them at all. With the support of the American Red Cross, the Army even segregated blood plasma donated by whites and blacks. Consider the irony in that, the method used for preserving plasma was perfected by Dr. Charles R. Drew, a black man.

World War Two brought the conflict of the seas and the battlefields squarely to the homefront: to the kitchen, the living room, the schools, shops and theaters. Every home- body was reminded almost every hour of every day that War was raging somewhere. We knew it from air-raid drills, coping with shortages, rationing, planting Victory gardens, buying War Bonds, scrap metal drives, and absorbing heavy doses of propaganda with our entertainment. War Time (now called Daylight Saving Time) went into effect for the duration. Wake-up time for families became 6 a.m. instead of 7 a.m. Folks had to be at work *on time*. After all: "There was a war on." Gasoline and tires were rationed which meant the use of packed buses, trolleys and trains to get places, including the workplace. With rationing, diets were healthy but not necessarily hearty. Food rationing rules practically gave housewives enough experience at juggling cookbooks and checkbooks to sit for their state's CPA exam. In a nutshell, the system worked like this: Each individual received two ration books. One had blue coupons for canned goods, the other contained red coupons for meat, fish and dairy products. Each person was allotted 48 blue points and 64 red points per month. A housewife shopping for canned goods for a family of four had a total of 192 points to use however she chose. At the start of a new month everyone got new ration stamps—and new sets of figures to juggle. Reflecting the availability of foods, applesauce took 10 points in March, 1943 and climbed to 25 in March a year later—while grapefruit juice dropped from 23 to 4 during the same period. Ration stamps were like gold. Although creating major headaches for all concerned, rationing was regarded as yet another notch to carve in the belt called "freedom at any price."

Most housewives and mothers were *working* wives and mothers. With the men at war, jobs for women were simply for the asking. In offices and factories people pulled together like never before. Loafing on the job was a no-no, as was petty griping and the standard office intrigue. Besides, there wasn't time. Everybody put in maximum hours on the job. The country was at war; the jobs were many and had to get done. Complaints about poor work, slow service or sub-quality products usually earned the inevitable surly rejoinder from overworked staff: "Don't you know there's a war on?" Americans at home accepted a degree of discipline and government interference in their lives that would not have been tolerated in peacetime. Roosevelt's administration continued in the vein of "alphabetic regulation" carried over from the Depression years. There was the OPA—Office of Price Administration, OWI—Office of War Information, and OCD—Office of Civilian Defense, *et al.* The OCD was the principle governing body aimed at channeling the energies on the home front into the War effort. Fiorella H. La Guardia, Mayor of New York City, was its first director. He called on each American to "give an hour a day for the U.S.A." The OCD encouraged everyone to take first-aid training. As a result the best-selling book of 1942 was the *Red Cross First Aid Manual.*

Scrap drives collected everything from gum wrappers to old rubber galoshes to tin cans. Scrap paper was the easiest to come by. A national paper drive by the Boy Scouts in 1942 was so successful it glutted paper mills and had to be temporarily halted. Income taxes and the sale of War Bonds were the federal government's instruments to pay for World War Two. A five percent surcharge was imposed on all income taxes. It was called a "Victory Tax," supposedly to make it more palatable. The Treasury Department, at the same time, began requiring employers to deduct an appropriate percentage from workers earnings as income tax. Prior to this time, income taxes had been paid once a year. This was the beginning of the withholding tax. At a time when it was vitally needed, therefore, the Treasury's pay-as-you-go plan increased cash flow to government coffers to pay for the War. War Bonds and War Stamps were on sale everywhere—at school, at work, in movie theaters. Huge bond rallies were held throughout the country featuring major entertainment and sports celebrities of the day. Betty Grable's stockings and Man o' War's horseshoes were auctioned off. Actress Hedy Lamarr kissed anyone who bought $25,000 worth of bonds. Jack Benny's $75 violin—"Old Love in Bloom"—went for a million dollars at a Gimbel's bargain basement bond auction. Kate Smith, the popular singer and radio personality, was the champion seller with $40 million in pledges called in during a 16 hour network radio marathon.

The single, biggest sacrifice during those War years of lost freedoms was rationing and price controls. Our government deemed it a necessary evil in order to keep inflation down and to fairly distribute scarce goods. Rationing covered some twenty essential items from gasoline to tomato ketchup, coffee and shoes. The first item rationed nationwide was sugar. In May, 1942, Americans lined up at local schools and gave depositions to teachers and other volunteers as to how much sugar each consumer had at home. They were then issued ration coupons good for a 52-week supply. Practically in record time, housewives purses were cluttered with ration stamps—red for this, blue for that. The hoarding of war-critical food and material was prevented by coding the stamps for redemption within a specific period of time—usually a month. Meat rationing was complicated. It was affected by the type of cut and availability. On average, each person was allowed two pounds of meat per week. Gasoline rationing was even more elaborate. Each motorist received a windshield sticker with a pre-assigned priority letter from A to E. An A sticker was for pleasure driving only, good for one stamp and three to five gallons per week. Commuters got a B sticker, worth varying gas amounts based on distance from work. The E sticker was highest priority and reserved for emergency situations. It was assigned to policemen, clergymen and, occasionally, politicians. The E sticker brought as many gallons as needed. Farmers were also granted unlimited amounts of gasoline, but they paid for it in the tons of paperwork required by the government to justify it. Rationing was complicated and cumbersome. Presided over by the OPA, it was a true accountant's nightmare.

Liquor was in short supply. Alcohol was needed in explosives. Real whiskey left the scene at a time when wartime jitters and booming wages had increased the rate of hard drinking by 30 percent. People accepted going without butter because there was a war on. When they couldn't get whiskey, they raised hell. Clothing fashions changed due to shortages. Patched apparel became a fad since it indicated patriotic sacrifice. Men wore "Victory suits"—one pair of pants, narrow lapels, short jackets, no vests or cuffs. Women wore skirts one inch above the knee—an OPA decree—and two-piece swimming suits. Women's legs were bare. The silk from stockings went to make parachutes. Leg make-up came into vogue. An application of the so-called "bottled stockings" would last three days with luck and no baths. Some women even used an eyebrow pencil to create the illusion of a stripe down the back of the leg. The major problem that men had with "bottled stockings" was summed up in a popular song: "It decants on your pants."

Military production and construction throughout the country created boom-towns and housing shortages. Landlords rented so-called "hot beds" to workers for eight hours at 25 cents. News of empty space anywhere instantly created a rush to move in. Newspaper obits were scanned religiously in search of available lodgings. One situation involved a man in New York City who fell from the Staten Island Ferry and caught the attention of a fellow passenger with his cries for help.

"What is your name and where do you live?" demanded the passenger.

"John Smith, 27 South Maple Street—Help!" the drowning man gasped frantically.

The passenger immediately rushed to that address and excitedly told the landlady: "I want to rent John Smith's room. He just drowned."

"Sorry," replied the landlady, "it was just taken by the man who pushed him in."

During the war years most business establishments increased their net worth by an average of 40 percent. After enduring the ravages of the 1930s Great Depression, suddenly rivers of spending money abounded. In other venues, the country's most basic institutions began showing some strain. Whirlwind romances produced a surge in weddings and, in 1943, the highest birth rate in two decades—thanks to the boom in "good-bye babies." Divorce doubled over pre-war figures. By 1943, female to male alcoholism increased from 1 in 5 to 1 in 2. Infidelity was a constant source of stress for husbands and wives. Teenagers became highly independent during the early 1940s: Family life was less structured; easy money abounded; radical clothing styles evolved (the zoot suit); an old dance—the Lindy, with a new name—the jitterbug, had practically every teenager "cutting a rug" or, as older, less agile, wet blankets put it: "performing a mating dance with emulations of sexual foreplay." Huh? A very young and very skinny singer from Hoboken, NJ, Frank Sinatra, got most of the blame for the new wartime teenage craze. His appearance at Manhattan's Paramount Theater in 1944 caused a near riot by 30,000 teenage girls (bobby-soxers). They almost strangled him by his own bow tie. Once, when he sang "I'll Walk Alone," a female voice from the audience cried out in Brooklynese: "I'll walk wid ya, Frankie!"

Sinatra was blamed unfairly for much of the current teen-age delinquency in America. In retrospect, most experts now agree that the wartime breakdown in family permanence— working mothers, absent fathers, boomtowns and worldwide violence—was the more logical explanation for the sudden digression in young morals. At the height of the War, certain teen-age girls loafed around drugstores and bus depots where servicemen on leave were known to congregate. They were known variously as "khakiwacky," "Victory girls" and "patriotutes." Out of a totally voluntary, yet misguided, sense of patriotism, they showed an almost spellbound willingness to surrender their bodies to any man in uniform. Females serving on active duty, for other reasons, were tacitly urged to exercise selective "hanky panky." The Navy suggested to it's WAVES Battalion: *If you're going to have sex, do it with a sailor; he's as clean as you are.*

There was scarcity in the land of plenty. Americans at home were mandated to drive their cars at a 35-mph speed limit to conserve on gas and rubber. It was called "Victory Speed." Auto-makers stopped making family cars in 1942. Gas was rationed. Tires— including retreads—were scarce. New household appliances were not being made. Meat eaters survived on a ration of two pounds a week. Butter users got twelve pounds a year. Coffee drinkers had to get by on a cup a day, while the average sugar ration was less than a pound a week. Thirty percent of America's cigarette production went to the military.

Some Americans hoarded. Most Americans endured. They made do. They patched up the old cars, drove slow and shared the ride. Smokers rolled-their-own. Coffee drinkers re-brewed the grounds. Home heating fuel was rationed, resulting in an average in-house temperature of 65 degrees. Some, without houses, had tents for homes, or packing crates. Meat rationing hurt the most. Most housewives had money and ration coupons to spare, but nothing to buy except un-rationed horse, buffalo, antelope and beaver meat. *Gourmet* magazine, in an unusual moment, advised: Eat the Easter Bunny.

The War years described here[46] saw an extraordinary loss in personal, taken-for-granted freedoms. We survived. We got over it. Millions of us around today still remember when freedom was a fading memory and not even a certain hope to return. But as we return from and consider those unfair "future" days of yesteryear, we pause at 8:48 a.m., Tuesday, September 11, 2001. Oddly . . . it's War Time again. *The future is back.* It's not what was promised. We should be growing young with our grandchildren, video conferencing with them, and learning their computer skills. I hate to be morbid but after retirement the future is about obituaries and cremation and funerals. Not mine, of course, since I'll be staying on a spell until certain *arschlochen* get their well-deserved comeuppance. The future we talked of and predicted . . . it's upon us. We planned to have time to remember. It's what old folks do in the future anymore—*remember*, remember precisely where they were at certain times: Pearl Harbor, VJ Day, JFK's assassination . . . Twin Towers . . . er, I don't know what it's called yet. Does anybody? But they've destroyed our buildings . . . New York City . . . our future.

On September 12, 2001, our President called us to arms. Our legislators, parading before us day and night, displayed a marvelous facade of brotherly bipartisanship as they discussed the critical issues: national security; economic stimulus; when, how and where to wage war; anti-terrorism measures; biological warfare; racial profiling; immigration issues; constitutional law *vis a vis* the use of military and/or civilian courts; and other "down home" issues. Meanwhile, we, the citizenry, oozed patriotism and went bonkers in search of enough flags to wave. Our national pep rally lasted about three weeks. As the "hurrahs" began fading, happily the flag waving stayed, as did a huge lot of pent up patriotism in heretofore, silent citizens. The President's poll numbers were through the roof. The congressional *left* needed to make a move, and did—egged along by the usual liberal media "giants" schooled in the "no news is bad news, bad news is good news" affliction. After deciding that nothing was happening, Democratic leaders questioned the President's inaction while demanding action: "With all that's happened and all the 'rah, rah, rah', what's happening? And where's the plan? If there is a plan, where's our copy to leak to the media? For God's sake, Mr. President, how long does it take to start a war against nomads with camels and caves? It's been a month, now! Betcha we look like fools in front of the world. Those Taliban guys in Kabul prob'ly are laughin' their turbans off." When the war was eventually underway, the complaints kept coming: "Fer Chrissake! It's been six weeks now since we dropped the first bomb and we haven't won yet. We need ground troops in there. . . . hit 'em with ever'thing. What kind o' government we plannin' for over there? Where do we attack next, Mr. President? . . . and who, Mr. President? Isn't anybody at the White House doing anything???" As December arrived the bloom was completely off the rose. Hillary Clinton talked—seriously—of hearings to resolve the "dignity and liberation from male bondage" problem of the down-trodden, Afghan female—a situation, till then, ignored by American feminist groups; but a condition—by some stretch of abnormal thought—for which Hillary seemed prepared to remedy and take full credit in the name of the United States of Clinton. Inevitably criticism returned to the President's earlier miniscule $40 billion dollar tax cut, as the Dems blamed that legislation for destroying the economy. Hillary chimed in again: "If we hadn't passed the big tax cut last spring, that I believe undermined our fiscal responsibility and our ability to deal with this new threat of terrorism, we wouldn't be in the fix we're in today."[47] In an added comment, she suggested as to how her *impeached* (my word) husband's carry-over policies would have championed the day. This from a woman who a few years earlier probably thought that a "cattle future" was an unborn heifer. Now, curiously, she's charging the President of the United States with a failed fiscal policy. Does anyone here take Basic Economics, anymore?

Next, the media stormed the airways with an "around-the-clock" bulletin, proclaiming a universal anthrax epidemic. Four anthrax deaths out of, roughly, twenty-four reported cases was practically hailed as akin to the Black Death of year 1347 which wiped out half of Europe. The anthrax deaths—a tragedy, yes—were in no way a major disaster. Media types played precisely into the hands of would-be perpetrators with maximum coverage to a relatively innocuous situation. And, how about the economic "stimulus" package? Democrats declared the best way to stimulate economic growth was by increasing unemployment benefits, as well as adding a little pork to the package for millionaire buffalo ranchers out west, to name one such benefactor. Needless to say this line of thinking immediately got them onto the President's *"fecal roster"* as Mr. Bush threatened a veto on anything less than "real stimulus." Senator Leahy got onto his high podium to disparage the administration's stand on the use of military tribunals to prosecute non-citizen terrorists. Senator Leahy intimated as to how the President didn't know "chocolate sherbet from Shinola" when it came to understanding the U.S.Constitution and protecting the rights and due process of the human race. I am still hoping that the President may set-up a new presidential web site for continuing falderal and blather yet to come. Call it: www.lifeisnotabowlofcherries.getoverit.com.

Then, in a short matter of time, the ACLU, America's Completely Ludicrous Union, made it back to the news hour by upholding the constitutionality of some State of Maryland legal buffoonery, i.e., (1) the banning of smoking in one's own home, and (2) barring Santa Claus from Christmas participation at local shopping malls. At the same time, they lock stepped with Senator Leahy's Committee on the administration's extreme treatment of foreign terrorists: Never mind that, daily, our "search and seizure" procedures were, and are, rummaging the personal belongings of mostly innocent air passengers. The true inequity is that we're harassing and messing with the "due process"—questionable at best—of alien, imprisoned, terrorists. . . . Folks, the wackos are still running the asylum! Sometimes I seriously think that they're pulling our collective, American leg. What a "revoltin' development" it really is now . . . etc . . . etc . . . *ad dementia!*

There are the marginal patriots among us who extol an ideology that says: *"Notwithstanding my un-interest, through inevitability this too shall pass."* Do they ever come to the balanced sense that freedom in America is not a gift from the ACLU, but a Bill of Rights from long ago for all citizens—with or without the fear of God. And that it is acquired by duty to country and self, and far too elusive and precious to be placed in the heedless hands of Civil Libertarians? In its time, year 1945, had the Nuremberg, Germany, International War Crimes Tribunal been conducted in the style of a typical, modern day American civilian court trial, we'd still be selecting the jury.

As it is influenced, therefore, by a veracious and moral majority, may the future be with you and you with it. As for the real future, a piece of us all will be forever in "A New York State of Mind."[48]

Chapter Fourteen

The AARP Be With You: R.I.P Uncle Bob

    Forgive this senior moment: I love old folks; mainly, because I am one. But as a forgotten Jimmy Van Heusen lyric asks: "Where Did Everyone Go?" The song dolefully relates the impotent spirit of lost youth, friends and life . . . of simply being over the hill for good. The words weave a poignant tale of a former *bon vivant*, a "hale fellow, well-met" gent who long ago confidently owned his own little "piece of the rock." Health, wealth, social position, acclaim: he'd known them all. To make it sweeter, he'd enjoyed the exclusive company of a twenty-four carat lady. But in a bittersweet remembrance, he confides that all has been lost:

"Remember, how I'd walk in? What excitement there would be.
Never less than twenty people, I had lots of friends you see.
I gave the party, I was the host; everyone loved me, I was the most.
Champagne and plenty of it, real imported caviar,
And the hat check girl got 'fifty', just for lighting my cigar.

I kept them laughing, jokes by the yard; everyone loved me, I was a card.

And I had a girl, a beautiful girl.

Her whole world, I think, consisted of mink, and diamonds and pearls.

Because she was mine, I'd glitter and shine.

And life was a ball. And wasn't it all so cozy and fine?

But nothing lasts forever. And the deepest well runs dry.

Just 'cause I stopped rolling sevens doesn't mean I have to cry.

I'll take that nightcap. One more won't show. And incidentally, maybe you know.

Where? Oh, where? Oh, where, did everyone go?"[49]

"The sweet bird of youth soon flies away, and nothing can make him stay."[50]

The American Association of Retired Persons loves old "birds," too; mainly because they know an easy mark with ready cash. It's the unsuspecting senior geezers who fall legal prey to these AARP people. First off, they scare the living hell from you with subtle predictions of personal and political reversals. Then comes the next pitch and how with a little help from *your* stagnating, senior citizen bank account, they—AARP—can shield you nicely from the ravages of medical malpractice, financial scams, insurance fraud and old age. All it takes is the time for your good money to reach their bulging coffers. From then on, life as you knew it—with their guidance and your funding—is to be miraculously preserved in perpetuity. Your remaining earthly tenure is to be the aura of golden days. In reality you have just joined one of the largest, liberal government lobbies in existence. Lists, with your name included, are routinely sold off and bandied about the free world. Instantly you're getting junk mail—about a ton a day—shoveled through your mail slot, promising entitlements for the rest of your natural life and beyond. Things like long-term health care to be financed by the monsters of the tobacco industry. Forget that our liberal legal system is hell bent to see all "money-grubbing capitalists" out of business. Prescription drug costs will be taxed to the rich and to those mysterious non-working families somewhere (as opposed to "working class families everywhere" that modern liberal leaders mention in hushed reverence). After all this benevolence is digested, what's it worth, really, but a lousy subscription to a magazine and a discount card. With the card you get rebates already earned because already you're listed in some giant national registry as a genuine sixty-five year old "seasoned" citizen?

When rarely asked, my advice on senior support groups is: Shop around. . . . The United Seniors Association is out there, too. . . . Not as loud or showy as AARP . . . less liberal . . . and a lot sensible. In my dotage I prefer conservative. It's very much the way our country was in the old days. Liberal is okay. It's not a crime yet. If you're going to be a liberal, though, step down from your high-brow stance and make your cause "true charity of heart and mind" for the true good of the common man. Avoid being tagged a liberal, uttering "sound without sense"—*vox et praeterea nihil.* Consider that "the voice of the people is the voice of God"—*vox populi, vox Dei.* Fight conservative opposition with better ideas. Stop shooting the messenger. Be a problem solver . . . not the problem. Try getting tomorrow's weather right two days in a row before crowing about environmental issues. That done, it may be perfectly okay to blithely toss into the mix dire threats of global warming and the end of civilization in the next one hundred years. If you're really serious about endangered species, start hanging out with the very young, old and poor. Let genuine idiots worry on the plight of the elusive, vanishing snail darter and sucker fish. Most modern liberals got their "liberal values" from around 1965. Most living seniors with a liberal "bent" got theirs from the 1920s or 1930s. It wasn't liberalism then. It was more of a "progressive conservatism." Thinking back to President Kennedy's term in office (1960-1963) and had he lived into the twenty first century, today he could easily fit in as a moderate conservative Republican. If the modern liberal movement's "intelligentsia" continues to rule rather than respond to mainstream America's innate curiosity and other realities of the conscious mind, one day soon we'll be exactly far enough *left* to put our world into socialistic hock for eternities yet to come. It's a stale line, but we really do need statesmen, not politicians. As the year 2000 presidential election night ended, our sacred national spirit lay in the throes of the greatest divisive onslaught against a majority of Americans—including seniors—since the American Civil War. AARP was right in there pushing the agenda of most liberal legislators, with their threatened loss of Social Security and Medicare as their major political scare tactic. Also, lest we seniors forget, in 1993 it was Clinton tax policy that put Social Security benefits into the highest tax bracket in U.S. history. Politicians have been talking tax cuts for *all*. All, that is, except American taxpayers collecting Social Security benefits. AARP peddles their Medicare supplement program as the finest device since squirtless grapefruit because their rates never change. It's the truth. They enroll you, day one, at the highest price on the chart. They hawk their wares to members at top rates, all the while sounding like street urchins gathering crumbs for survival through the winter. Liberal Democratic rhetoric gave the term "special interest group" a bad rap as being a conservative plot to strangle the spirit and initiative of *good working families everywhere*. There's that baloney again: the implication that America's national work ethic arose from the bowels of the land by the sweat, blood and suffering and unceasing struggles of our earliest ancestors as they grew and evolved into loyal Democrats, liberals and Americans. AARP is one of the largest, well-heeled special interest groups in the country, with major lobbying facilities on both coasts . . . and it sure ain't run by conservatives. It's not even run by seniors. AARP endures the advice of "senior advisors." Big deal! Through the retirement years AARP may be adequate on issues recreational, medical and spiritual. Keep them out of your pocket book! Shop around!

It sounds farfetched but the day could arrive when AARP reaches out and actually befriends the entire elder generation. It'll be a day when some "knowing" whackos in our midst conclude a study confirming the *good sense* of the Dutch and Scandinavians in the matter of senior euthanasia. To put seniors out of their misery would be deemed a *saving grace* and become a *reasonable* issue and start making *perfectly good sense* to some future legislative generation—like the good sense of abortion and ending the death penalty. In a battle to save their bottom—nonprofit—line, AARP will fight through that dire dilemma to see all seniors live . . . and pay another day; pay, possibly, through the good auspices of a future, new and exciting AARP spin-off: the SPCSC—Society for the Prevention of Cruelty to "you know who."

Lots of folks I know and meet these days are part of the senior citizenry. Two varieties exist. Ninety-nine percent are exactly as the name implies: (1) Senior, as in superior, of great dignity, more advanced, etc. (2) Citizen, as in resident, taxpayer, voter, etc. These are not folks to toy with. As to the other one percent, you can always catch their act. Go, on any given Senior Citizen Sales Day, to any participating crowded store, in any part of this great land. They stand out. Look to the nearest check-out counter for some little, old man or lady—or both—behind the handle of possibly the largest shopping cart available in the free world. The basket usually contains two items—denture adhesive and cat food—as, with NASCAR adroitness, they maneuver the thing for "pole position" like A. J. Foyt (or, for a few, Barney Oldfield) at the Indy 500.

What's the big deal about waiting in a check-out line? Many seniors consider it time well spent. Lay back! Get to know your fellow checkee! You'll be richer for it! You'll hold onto your money longer. Talk to someone about something—social security, or unsocial security. Be daring. Be a show stopper—try whistling the "Minute Waltz" in thirty seconds. You may get applause; you probably will not. Ask about the family—so what if you don't know them from Adam . . . or Eve! Don't forget the weather, the latest scores. How about the mess in the world (if you have lots of time)? Give someone, heaven forbid, a compliment. Just open your mouth for God's sake! You could drop dead at the head of the line with no last words uttered for posterity . . . worse than wearing dirty underwear. So talk about anything! Many will ignore you. Who cares? Why the embarrassment? Who's gonna' remember a hundred years from today? But, for crying out loud, whatever you do, stop the damned running and bumping into everyone and trying to break the sound barrier by being first through the line and out to the parking lot and into your car to get somewhere you probably didn't need to be for at least another hour. Be charitable. Next time in a check-out line—be it supermarket, drug store, or any store—smile. Step to the back. Let someone move ahead. You could make a new friend. You probably will not. But you'll feel great and love yourself for it, . . . maybe.

I love what AARP says it can do for me. Someday I'll check it out. Meanwhile, inside this fat and frail body resides the heart and mind of a boy. I've said it before. I love old folks. I am one. I also love young folks and middle aged folks and kids and octogenarians, Rotarians, Philadelphians (oops . . . I'll have a rain check on that one). But gim'me a break. When certain folks reach their so-called *golden years*, they suddenly turn into a circus of stumble-bum loonies waiting for the gravy train to pull into Penn Station with freebies *ad nauseam* for all. And where do they say it's all coming from? Naturally! From AARP! Excuse me and gim'me another break!

AARP has influenced the creation of some great things for the senior generations. Does anybody even know how much? It's written that if every program ever proposed by AARP's national lobby actually became law, the Federal government would triple in size. Honestly folks, I refuse to be part of that kind of growth. It's stupid. Instead, let's all of us get behind the programs that will support our children and grandchildren. Why should they have to support us? Since the mid-1960s there has been growing among us a brotherhood of ignoble, so-called statesmen. Insidiously, this great country has been led, willingly and in ignorance, into the morass of a moral skid row. Millions of seniors—regardless of political preference—based solely on moral grounds, disagree with America's direction during the last thirty-five years. Putting the national economic question aside, since prosperity and recession are the results of various uncontrollable factors in any year, honest confrontation, today, on vital issues is not the treasonous act that some would have you believe. In truth, nothing about disagreement seems civil anymore, particularly when aimed at liberal "sacred cows." Seniors are intimidated on the issues by veiled warnings that entitlement programs—Medicare or Social Security—may dry up. Political perpetrators like AARP even throw a non-existent prescription drug program into the act. The *myth* of a prescription drug entitlement has been talked up for so many years, I suspect that more than a few seniors actually believe a viable program is already in place. Furthermore, if as honest citizens we disagree on certain targeted senior issues, then by default we're accused by some of selling out fellow seniors, or assumed to lack compassion and be mean spirited. In other words, we should just generally go to hell and stay put. For most genuine senior citizens still alive and serving in the years after 2001, life started with the Great Depression and segued into World War II and the Korean Conflict. Thanks to help from the G.I.Bill most of us got an education, landed a decent job and lived happily ever after until about 1964. Now, after thirty-some years of finally dissipating into the "no man's land" of modern liberalism, despite our noble beginnings and aspirations, many families feel dependent and compelled at the end of life's journey to pay homage to the seeming *magnanimity* of AARP. Hovering behind the scenes at the final "senior moment" of every departed citizen, as each gets a couple "C notes" from Social Security to defray the cost of covering their rotting flesh with a load of dirt, AARP's pervasive presence everywhere almost evokes the notion that the money came from them. Heaven forbid, we should waste a nano second and withhold the wisdom of this group from our final years. Like insurance men and bankers—fair weather friends all—AARP's promise to see us through life's last grand experience is easily mistaken for some ethereal, angelic bash at Camelot with Perceval and Galahad, discussing a *divvy up* of The Holy Grail.

I remember my old Uncle Bob. Like many of his era, he never worried about missing the largesse of AARP. He had greater regrets. As a young man he was a pretty fair baseball player. He died at ninety-seven—joyful in his many accomplishments, remorseful to leave a loving family in the distress of grief—only lamenting in life an inability to execute a perfect bunt on the suicide squeeze.

What a guy! What a generation! *What a bunch of winners!*

NOTES

1 "Nothing New Beneath the Sun" Words and music by George M. Cohan. (1906)

2 Greek proverb

3 Thomas Carlyle, "The Opera" (1852)

4 "And Then Some." Recorded by Bob Crosby Band for Decca, July, 1935. Owned or controlled by BMG Music. All rights reserved.

5 William Shakespeare, 2 Henry IV (1597-98)

6 Thomas Wolfe, *Thomas Wolfe's Letters to His Mother* (1943)

7 Edward Young, *Night Thoughts* (1742-46)

8 Flappers 2 Rappers by Tom Dalzell. Merriam-Webster, Inc. (1996)

9 A reference to the German poem, "Die Lorelei" by Heinrich Heine. (1850)

10 Montaigne, "Of Experience," Essay., (1580-88)

11 "Brother, Can You Spare a Dime?," Music by Jay Gorney. Lyrics by E. Y. Harburg. (1932)

12 Editorial, *Intelligencer Journal*, Lancaster, PA. (April 5, 2001)

13 "Scoring big on Enron" by Chris Matthews, *San Francisco Chronicle*. (1/18/02)

14 Bruce Friedrich, PETA Spokesperson. July 3, 2001.

15 Patrick Moore, Greenpeace Co-Founder, describing his former organization.

16 Bryant Gumbel: Exchange during CBS "Early Show," April 18, 2001.

17 Excerpt from Stephen Moore, "The Daschle Deception." *Human Events*. Week of January 14, 2001.

18 Exchange on CNN's "Larry King Live," July 27, 2001.

19 Former UPI White House reporter Helen Thomas intro-

ducing Clinton at Greater Washington Society of Association Executives lecture shown on C-SPAN, October 9, 2001.

20 "Oh! Look at Me Now," Music by Joe Bushkin, lyrics by John DeVries (1941).

21 Nathaniel Hawthorne, *American Note-Books*, July 14, 1850

22 "Ya Got Trouble" from the stage play and movie, *The Music Man*. Words and music by Merideth Willson. (1957)

23 Spanish proverb.

24 "Movin, Out (Anthony's Song)", Words and music by Billy Joel (1977).

25 Movie skit by Red Skelton, "Guzzler's Gin," Ziegfield Follies. (1946)

26 "All-American Girl," Words and music by Al Lewis. (1932)

27 Excerpts from an article by Bob Greenberg, Sportscaster WBEZ, Chicago, IL and KMOX St. Louis, MO.

28 "Indians and Trees." Words and music by George M. Cohan. (1933)

29 "Paula Jones deposition," reported in *National Review*. (2/19/01)

30 Peter Collier & David Horowitz, "The Teamster Hearings," The Kennedys. (1984)

31 Peggy Noonan, "The Donkey in the Living Room," *The Wall Street Journal*. (11/17/00)

32 Maureen Dowd, "Breaking Up the Bush Monopoly," *The New York Times* (Reprint Lancaster, PA *Sunday News*. 11/19/00)

33 Lewis Carroll, "A Mad Tea-Party," *Alice In Wonderland* (1865)

34 Maureen Dowd, "Quiet As The Grave," *The New York Times* (Re-printed Lancaster, PA, *IntellJournal*, 9/16/0 1).

35 Chris Matthews, "Will President Bush Rise to the Challenges?", *San Francisco Chronicle* (Re-printed Lancaster, PA, *IntellJournal*, 9/15/01)

36 Lewis Carroll, "Jabberwocky", *Through The Looking Glass*. (1871)

37 "Swinging On A Star." Words by Johnny Burke. Music by Jimmy Van Heusen. (1944)

38 "Choo Choo Ch' Boogie." By V. Horton, M. Gabler & D. Darling (1945)

39 Oliver Wendell Holmes, St., "The Boys," (1809 - 1894)

40 *Compton's Interactive Encyclopedia*, The Learning Company, Inc. (1999)

41 Oliver Wendell Holmes, Jr., Speech Bar Association, Feb. 5, 1885.

42 Sir Arthur Wing Pinero, *The Second Mrs. Tanqueray* (1893).

43 "When Paw Was Courtin' Maw," by Jack Manus & Leonard Joy (1938-ASCAP).

44 Irving Brecher, *The Life of Riley* (1944).

45 "They're Either Too Young or Too Old" Words and music by Frank Loesser/Arthur Schwartz (1943)

46 "The Home Front: U.S.A.", Time-Life Books, Inc. (1978)

47 "Hillary Watch," *Human Events*. Week of November 19, 2001.

48 "A New York State of Mind." Words and music by Billy Joel (1975).

49 "Where Did Everyone Go?" Words and music by Jimmy Van Heusen,

50 "Sweet Bird of Youth." Words and music by Schroeder/Gold.

Printed in the United States
5845